THIS BELOVED ROAD

VOL. II

THIS
BELOVED
ROAD

VOL. II - Into the Source

AMY LAYNE LITZELMAN

www.AmyLayneLitzelman.com

This Beloved Road Vol. II
Copyright © 2014 by Amy Layne Litzelman. All rights reserved.

Published in the United States of America
ISBN: 978-0692284889
1. Religion, Christian Life, Devotional
2. Religion, Christian Life, Spiritual Growth

"What comes into our minds when we think about God
is the most important thing about us…

Worship is pure or base as the worshiper
entertains high or low thoughts of God."
A.W. Tozer[1]

Table of Contents

Foreword

"To know and not to do is really not to know."
Stephen R. Covey

When God wants to teach His sons something, He takes them for a walk. From the time of Adam to Enoch to Abraham and Moses, God has revealed Himself on the way to somewhere. Pilgrimages are at the heart of the Biblical witness because that is the vehicle God uses to raise His sons. Jesus said, "Follow me and I will make you fishers of men." A person learns by doing. The unveiling of God's nature, and consequently, the transformation of ours, takes place in the journey.

Along the way, one begins to see things and people through different eyes. Attitudes get challenged, prejudices exposed, and hearts unveiled. These are the places where altars are built, sacrifices are made, worship is offered, decisions are recorded, and Heaven answers. Transformation ensues through choices to let go of one way of understanding and to embrace another. The Lord's heart woos us into new revelation and understanding and the journey becomes more like a dance, an interface between heaven and earth.

It is the walking out of that experience that causes one to be known by God and gives one authority with God. True authority does not come from being powerful or gifted or witty or clever or charming. It comes from vulnerability. Your authority comes when you allow God to take you and shape you through the journey. God wants to write all of us into His story. But you have to "go there"; you have to take a walk with Him. There is no faking it. You cannot keep choosing your own way and still go with Him. You cannot keep your life. You have to let go of it in order to find it. Each one must choose to follow. And if you do, you will not remain unchanged.

My friend, Amy Layne Litzelman, is a woman who has been on a journey with God. She writes with beauty, wisdom, and grace as one who has experienced deep dealings from the Father. In these pages, Amy gives us more than a chronicle of her discoveries; she gives us the fragrance of meekness, a revelation of the heart of one who is being taught and instructed. She also offers us a profound vision of the kindness of God. Amy is more than a writer; she is a guide, extending her hand and offering you an invitation.

As you read these simple stories and truths, don't be afraid to release your heart and your trust into the care of the Father. He knows who you are and what you need. Put your hand in His. Volunteer your vulnerability and go on the journey. You will not be sorry.

Brian Harrison
August 24, 2014

A Far Greater Purpose

"I am torn between the two:
I desire to depart and be with Christ,
which is better by far;

but it is more necessary for you
that I remain in the body."
Philippians 1:23-24 (NIV)

Sometimes there are no words. Only silence. Silent pain. Silent disbelief. Silent horror. Silent prayer.

My husband, Matt, and I don't watch TV so I see far less news and entertainment than most, but often what I see or hear is enough to make me pause.

How does the earth hold up under the agony and torment of so many? How can billions of people do to themselves and each other what they do? The degree of manipulation and selfishness and suffering is staggering.

There have been days when my overwhelmed heart echoed Paul's words, "*I desire to depart and be with Christ, which is better by far.*"

Then a faint calling, deep to deep, captures me again. Through the dark smoke and shadows of this world a simple desire rises from my chest:

"I long, yes, I faint with longing to enter the courts of the Lord..." Psalm 84:2 (NLT)

Then I realize my longing is not so much to leave this world as to step back in the midst and enter into His peace,

His presence, His wisdom. I long to hear His thoughts, gain His perspective, and feel His touch. I long to live from *God's* Kingdom, not the kingdoms of this world. And in that, to release it wherever I go.

At times we forget: Heaven unleashed its Kingdom on earth the day Jesus rose from the grave.

- Light overcame darkness.
- Life defeated death.
- Joy overruled mourning.
- A Rock stood firm through the storm.

We're not here just to change policies or make laws or argue opinions.

We're here for a far greater purpose: To release hope. To speak truth. To love beyond ourselves. As children of the King, we're called to bring His Kingdom to a hurting world. A hurting neighbor. A hurting soul. We are here to see the dead come to Life.

But we must realize the Kingdom of Heaven doesn't increase by accident or mere activity.

The flow of Kingdom Life through you is directly related to the depth and purity of your relationship with the King, Jesus.

The Holy Spirit spoke this word of direction in a recent journal entry:

> *"Do not be afraid or discouraged.*
> *I will strengthen you Myself.*
> *You are learning to overcome evil with good.*
> *You are being trained as a warrior of Love.*
>   (See Romans 12:21)*

> *Take heed, lest you stumble.*
> *Keep your focus on Me, not the surroundings.*

To overcome you must be focused on
and connected to the Overcomer."

Don't you love when the Holy Spirit brings you back to the bottom line?

We have nothing to give of lasting value, save Him. We cannot hope to bring hope without His grace pouring through us. We cannot love without the King of love renewing our mind and changing us into His image. And yet, as we set our gaze upon Him, He will strengthen us to overcome evil with good.

Father, fill me again with Your love. Fill and consume me with Your Spirit. Live through me that others may know the beauty and power of Your Son. That others may find the freedom and healing their souls cry out for. You are worthy. You are worthy.

A God Who Gives

"For God so greatly loved
and dearly prized the world
that He [even] gave…"
John 3:16 (AMP)

I often find myself torn in the weeks leading up to Christmas.

I'm stunned that the perfect imprint and very image of God's nature – the One who upholds and maintains and guides and propels the universe by His mighty word of power – would lie in a bed of hay as a crying babe. (See Hebrews 1:3 AMP.)

I can't help but wonder as I recall John the Baptist leaping in Elizabeth's womb at the mere sound of Mary's greeting.

And my chest is gripped each time I read Mary's passionate exchange:

"My soul magnifies and extols the Lord, and my spirit rejoices in God, my Savior… He has filled and satisfied the hungry with good things…" Luke 1:46-47; 53 (AMP)

The details of a young virgin giving birth, a young bridegroom persuaded by an angel, a group of shepherds chosen as the first visitors – these never get old or dusty. I'm overwhelmed by such love and grace.

But as much as I want to focus fully on this most important Gift, I find myself with stockings stuffed and boxes under the tree and I wonder how I can stray from the true meaning of Christmas.

Every year I think we're going to get our sons a few small gifts. But each year my husband, Matt, and I long to give our best: something to touch their hearts and fulfill their needs. I get so excited thinking of their excitement and surprise, but then feel guilty as presents pile up.

A few days ago I read something written by a good friend, Steve: *"The giving of gifts during Christmas is a good thing because each gift we receive prophetically speaks of a much greater gift we have been given."*

And I began to ponder.

Is it wrong to give gifts to those I love? Am I too focused on the world when I share what I have? *Or am I representing the heart of One who gave the greatest Gift?*

Giving is the heart of my Father.

He gave His Son in that manger because He wanted the best for you, for me. Because He wanted to fulfill our needs.

But mostly, He gave to satisfy His own intense love for us.

> "But God – so rich is He in His mercy! Because of *and* in order to satisfy the great *and* wonderful *and* intense love with which He loved us…made us alive together in fellowship *and* in union with Christ…"
> Ephesians 2:4-5 (AMP)

These verses stun me every time I read them. That you and I would be the focus of so much love.

As I pondered these words again, I realized a very important truth: When we give out of love, we are agreeing with the image of God in us. It's when we *don't* long to give that we need to step back and say, *"Father, change my heart."*

This Christmas, go ahead. Pour out your love in deep and intense and wonderful ways.

In words.

In actions.
In gifts.

Let the beauty of giving reveal a Father who so greatly loves and dearly prizes us that He gave His best.

A Jellyfish?

"For ever since the creation of the world
His invisible nature *and* attributes, that is,
His eternal power and divinity,
have been made intelligible *and* clearly discernible
in *and* through the things that have been made..."
Romans 1:20 (AMP)

In an ice-breaker, I was asked to tell what I'd choose if I could be any animal.

I'd never given much thought to this question before so was surprised when *jellyfish* came to mind. I argued with myself for a minute before trusting the Holy Spirit's prompting.

Later when I did a little research, I read this:

"Jellyfish drift along the water currents and depend on wind, tides, and ocean currents for horizontal movement, but are capable of vertical movement."

Yes! That's what I want to be – able to go up into my Father's presence, but dependent upon the currents and wind of His Spirit to direct how I connect with those around me.

I love that! I love how the Spirit of God knows what I want to be even more than I do and reveals it to me in the most unexpected ways.

This is the God we serve. This is our sovereign Creator. He knows you to your depths and His plans for you are good. He doesn't want to hamper your potential or keep you from what you love. He is unfolding it to you, perfectly.

Oh, Father. Lead us today in ways seen and ways unseen. Let us recognize Your love, wisdom, and power as You reveal Your plans for us. They are perfect. You are perfect.

All Things Beautiful

"The Spirit of God, who raised Jesus from the dead, lives in you.

And just as God raised Christ Jesus from the dead,
he will give life to your mortal bodies
by this same Spirit living within you."
Romans 8:11 (NLT)

Where would I be –
What would I be –
Who would I be – without Your love?

All things beautiful, all things good,
All things worthy – they come from You.

Where would I go –
What would I do –
Who would I know – without Your love?

Everything I want, everything I need,
Everything I love – I've found in You!

Blessed be Your name!
Blessed be Your name!
Blessed be Your name – O my God!

Everything I want, everything I need,
Everything I love – I've found in You!

A New Look at the Armor of God

"A final word:
Be strong in the Lord and in his mighty power.

Put on all of God's armor
so that you will be able to stand firm
against all strategies of the devil."
Ephesians 6:10-11 (NLT)

I've read Paul's description of the armor of God many, many times, but it recently struck me in a new way.

In the past, putting on the armor was more of a mental exercise: speaking or thinking the scripture and picturing myself putting on each piece. Although this exercise has its purpose and place, I believe these verses go much deeper.

I don't think Paul had mental exercises in mind when he exhorted the Body of Christ to gird itself with truth, put on the shoes of peace, and lift up a shield of faith.

The armor Paul described grows and expands as we mature in our spiritual walk.

Take the belt of truth, for example. Exactly how does truth protect us? It's not so much by just believing truth exists, but by knowing and holding to what is true in the midst of the battle.

I remember a life-changing conversation with my son, Sam, when he was a teenager. We discussed the difference between truth and fact. In the dictionary, they mean basically the same thing. But to those of us who are in Christ Jesus, they become distinctively different.

Facts are all around us and perceived with our five senses. The fact is many people are hurting and hungry, enslaved in addictions and circumstances. The fact is the world is full of unanswered questions and unsolved problems. The fact is we all know someone who is sick, even dying, and many who don't have hope for a future.

But in the midst of these facts stands truth.

The *truth* is God's perspective. The truth is God's plans. The truth is God's love, faithfulness, and Word. And truth always triumphs over facts.

Jesus lived a life of consistently bringing the truth of God into the facts around Him, and the facts changed.

When we put on the belt of truth, we don't just do a mental exercise. Instead, it is a daily walking out of the truths of the Word in trials and joys, and coming to know they are indeed irrefutable.

When we put on truth, we turn our gaze away from the facts around us, choosing instead to stand firmly on the character and faithfulness of our God. We feed our hearts and minds with the Word and the testimony it manifests before us. We hold onto it in spite of feelings or opinions, believing God's love, wisdom, and power cannot fail.

Jesus said in John 8:31-32: If we obey His teachings, we will know the truth and the truth will set us free. Free from what? Free from the lies and snares of Satan. Free from fear and anxiety. Free from confusion and doubt.

Truth takes us from the realm of earth's impossibilities into the realm of heaven's possibilities. Truth releases joy in the midst of pain and hope in the midst of darkness. Truth opens the door for the conquering Life of Christ. *This* truth covers and protects us.

Putting on the armor of God is an amazing journey of growth.

Putting on God's armor is walking in truth, pursuing peace, embracing righteousness and salvation, immersing ourselves in the Word, and growing in faith. It is coming to know the One who *is* our armor.

When we put on God's armor, we desire one thing: the fullness of Christ active in us.

A New Twist on Pruning

"So I ask you not to lose heart
[not to faint or become despondent through fear]
at what I am suffering in your behalf.
[Rather glory in it] for it is an honor to you.

For this reason [seeing the greatness of this plan
by which you are built together in Christ],
I bow my knees before the Father
of our Lord Jesus Christ,"
Ephesian 3:13-14 (AMP)

I remember the first time I helped prune a tree.

Disproportionate and stuffed into an alcove at the back of a home, you could hardly recognize what type of tree it was, let alone what might be growing in the bed beneath. I winced as large branches were cut off, sure we were removing too much. But to my surprise, an overgrown corner soon transformed into a beautiful shade garden.

This week as I pruned our aspen trees, I thought of the familiar teaching in John 15:

"I am the true grapevine, and my Father is the
gardener. He cuts off every branch of mine that
doesn't produce fruit, and he prunes the branches that
do bear fruit so they will produce even more." (v. 1-2,
NLT)

Pruning is widely recognized as an important step in the process for more fruit – with trees or in people. But as my pile of aspen branches grew taller, I realized the bushes and flowers beneath now had room to grow as well. Sunshine and water could better reach and nourish these smaller plants.

Here's my thought:

> Just as the low-hanging branches of my aspen trees hindered the growth of bushes and plants beneath, there may be things in our lives hindering the growth of those living close to us. When our Father God prunes us back – by His Word, by His Spirit, by the circumstances and people He puts in our lives – it not only causes growth and fruit in us, but greatly affects the growth in those around us.

Sometimes we get so focused on ourselves. We zero in on how we feel or how every bump in the road affects us.

But maybe the work God is doing in my life is *just* as much for those around me. Maybe the thing He's removing to allow more fruit in my own life will open up space for others to grow as well.

This excites me! It speaks again of the greatness of our God. It reminds me He is doing much more in each moment and circumstance than I can imagine, and all of it good.

Who sits in the shade of your life? Who has God positioned to grow with your encouragement, teaching, and protection?

Maybe your children, your spouse, or a Bible study group. Maybe someone you mentor or work with. Maybe you pastor a church or lead a large ministry. None of us walks alone.

Paul recognized the honor of suffering for the growth of the Body of Christ. He desired more than anything to know Christ and be conformed into His image. This required a lot of pruning. But the joy of seeing those around him display the wisdom of God was worth every trial, every test, every branch cut back.

"Every time I think of you, I give thanks to my God. Whenever I pray, I make my requests for all of you with joy, for you have been my partners in spreading the Good News about Christ from the time you first heard it until now.

And I am certain that God, who began the good work within you, will continue his work until it is finally finished on the day when Christ returns." Philippians 1:3-6 (NLT)

May we find joy in our Father's wisdom!

An Unequal Fight

"..in the middle of the lampstands
I saw one like a son of man,
clothed in a robe reaching to the feet,
and girded across His chest with a golden sash.

His head and His hair were white
like white wool, like snow;
and His eyes were like a flame of fire.

His feet *were* like burnished bronze,
when it has been made to glow in a furnace,
and His voice *was* like
the sound of many waters.

In His right hand He held seven stars,
and out of His mouth
came a sharp two-edged sword;
and His face was like the sun
shining in its strength.

When I saw Him,
I fell at His feet like a dead man..."
Revelations 1:13-17 (NASB)

Sometimes, even what we know we don't *fully* know.

John, author of the verses above, lived and walked daily with Jesus for three years. He laid his head upon Jesus' chest and spoke intimately with Him. He didn't doubt Jesus to be the Christ.

Even still, in a moment, a new revelation of his Savior and King caused John to melt.

Remember when Judas and the guards of the high priests and Pharisees came to arrest Jesus in the Garden? Jesus went out to them and asked, *"Whom are you seeking?"*

"Jesus the Nazarene," they answered.

Jesus merely spoke out, *"I am He,"* and they were thrown backwards and to the ground. (See John 18:1-6.)

Jesus didn't rise up with a sword against His enemy. He carried one in His mouth.

Eternal power encapsulated in words.

- As the world shakes around us,
- as darkness encroaches into areas we care about,
- as prophesies of old become realities of today,

I'm certain of one thing: There's no contest when it comes to Jesus and His enemies.

Jesus has been given all authority in heaven and on earth. (See Matthew 28:18.)

His hand isn't short or His arm weak. He's not sulking in a corner or hiding in a closet because of fear.

He's not worried or alarmed or even surprised.

Sometimes we act like we've forgotten how great He is. We look at the world around us in fear, even panic, and react as if God isn't great in our midst.

A verse recently lifted my perspective again. There will be a time when the antichrist, the lawless one, will be revealed. But in that revealing, our Savior will also be revealed and…

> "...the Lord Jesus will kill him with the breath of his mouth and destroy him by the splendor of his coming." II Thessalonians 2:8 (NLT)

By the breath of His mouth!

And the splendor of His coming!

This is the One we serve.
This is the One we love.
This is the Rock on which we stand.

May our eyes be opened to see Him more fully. And not just see, but rise up and walk in the authority and certainty He has purchased for us. There is *none* like our God.

A Witness

"You are My witnesses, says the Lord,
and My servant whom I have chosen,
that you may know Me, believe Me
and remain steadfast to Me,
and understand that I am He.

Before Me there was no God formed,
neither shall there be after Me.
I, even I, am the Lord,
and besides Me there is no Savior."
Isaiah 43:10-11 (AMP)

In the depths of despair, You are the Living River.
A drink, deep to deep.

You are my hiding place, my comfort, my hope.
You show me how bright Light is in the middle of the night;
how powerful Life is in the midst of death;
how freedom is found in a heavenly yoke.

You are the One who creates my hunger,
and the One who satisfies.

The One who strips away
and the One who rebuilds,
perfectly.

You are He who exposes the Father; who exposes my heart; who joins the two together regardless of time and space and loss.

The One who makes Love a person and this Person my Friend.

You tell me,

> *"Be strong and courageous!*
> *Don't be afraid!"*

When fear breathes fire in my face,
You hold my hand and smile,
confident in Your overcoming power, wisdom, and love.

You are the One who nudges me – in the middle of the night, in the routine of the day, in the words of others –

> *"Keep going. Don't quit. This is for My glory.*
> *For My glory in you. For My glory in them."*

You turn dark shadows into canopies of hope
and dry grass into gold.
My heart is spoiled and my breath consumed
when the beauty of earth
gives a glimmer of understanding
to the beauty of You.

You are the One who transforms average into amazing
and offers heaven to earth.

You bring what has always been
into the frame of time
for purposes eternal.

The grand and glitzy appear clumsy and worthless
in the light of Your purity.

You cause my heart to yearn for truth.
To yearn for You.

You are the One.
The One who has always been.
The One who will remain.

And You allow us to witness.

Can Prayer be a Distraction?

"For everything there is a season,
a time for every activity under heaven...

A time to tear down and a time to build up...

A time to be quiet
and a time to speak."
Ecclesiastes 3:1, 3, 7 (NLT)

Sometimes, what's obvious is not what's important.

2 am.

The puppy's barking. Matt jumps up to make it in time, to start this day as every other for the last month: a quick trip outside.

Ten minutes and everyone's settled back in. But like so many other nights I don't fall right to sleep.

So I sink back into my early morning time of prayer. I'm thankful for these quiet hours to agree with heaven.

Immediately my heart floods with thoughts of friends and family in the midst of difficulties and a world turned upside down with death and confusion. Even still, there's so much to thank my Father for. So many ways I see His mercy and love, His power and wisdom poured out.

I barely start when, like a gentle touch on the shoulder, the Holy Spirit stops me.

"Be still.
What do you hear?"

I pause.

"What do you feel?
Soak in this moment," He whispers.

As I lay still, little details each take their turn at center stage in the dark room.

- Rain gently pelting the roof and bouncing off windows.
- Wind chimes singing in harmony.
- Matt's measured breathing beside me. In. Out. In. Out.
- The soft, cool pillowcase under my neck.
- The weight of the comforter on my feet.
- The feel and sound of my own breath.

Remember that old saying, "Don't lose sight of the forest for the trees"? It's a reminder to not get so entangled with details and forget the big picture.

But what if we sometimes get so overwhelmed with the big picture and forget to enjoy the details?

Details set in place by the Master-Creator. Details pointing out where we stand and what's important. Details reminding us we're alive. Details declaring His glory.

This wasn't the Spirit's first invitation to lean back and savor the moment. They'd come over and over in recent weeks. Invitations to pause, to smile, to enjoy what might pass in the next breath.

- Moonlight through the clouds.
- Flavors that linger, sweet and spicy.
- Hugs that go deeper than skin.
- Dew in the morning and shadows making their way across afternoon hillsides.

As you know, there are two sides to every coin. Two points to every paradox.

> The One who said, "*Ask...seek...knock...*" (Matthew 7:7) also said, "*...your Father knows exactly what you need even before you ask him!*" (Matthew 6:8)

> The One who leads us to "*Pray without ceasing*" (I Thessalonians 5:17) also calls us to "*Be still...*" (Psalm 46:10)

Sometimes He just wants to hear the beat of your heart – and you to hear His.

Sometimes He waits until you let all else fade so you can feel His hand squeeze yours.

Sometimes your silent enjoyment of simple details gives Him greatest honor.

There are plenty of prayers to pray. Countless horizons to speak truth to. But take a moment. Take a few. And lean into the details. Lean into the sounds and rhythms and smells. Hold them close, even for a moment, and thank the One who gives you the ability to smile. He loves that.

Changing Your Perspective
on Obedience
(part 1)

"If you love Me,
obey My commandments."
John 14:15 (NLT)

Perspective can so easily get imbalanced.

Perhaps you learn something new and suddenly you believe this *one* thing is the answer to *everything*. Or maybe you refuse to alter a particular viewpoint even when new information comes to light because... well, change can be pretty uncomfortable.

Whether it's the latest craze in food and health, the newest of what technology has to offer, or the most recent scientific, political, or financial discovery, our pendulum seems to swing quickly to the extremes.

This can happen just as easily in our spiritual walk.

Maybe you hear a great teaching on trust and think everyone's problem is they just don't trust enough. Then you read a fantastic book on prayer and now everyone's issue is not praying enough.

It's easy to obsess on the latest topic rather than bringing it into the pool of what you already know.

Instead of swinging back and forth between individual points of truth, each piece we learn should build upon another to bring us closer to the full truth.

We all have so much to learn, no matter how much we know. Even after three years of living with and learning from

Jesus, the disciples still didn't know all there was to know. Jesus explained to them in John 16:

> "There is so much more I want to tell you, but you can't bear it now. When the Spirit of truth comes, he will guide you into all truth..." (v. 12-13, NLT)

Thankfully, the Holy Spirit still leads any who are willing into all truth. He's constantly unfolding the bigger picture to bring us into the full and accurate knowledge of God.

After a particular discussion, I was reminded of one area where I can get imbalanced: *intimacy with God* versus *walking in obedience*.

While my writing and teaching often focus on the joy of living in the secret place of God's love and presence, obeying His commandments is just as important. Our Creator designed us to live and walk in a divine combination of worship *and* obedience.

> "We need both reverence and obedience. If we worship but do not walk in obedience and discipline, we are emotional, lacking self-control and godly character. If we obey God's commandments but are not true worshipers, we become religious and judgmental. As the Pharisees in Jesus' day, we may miss the real meaning and purpose, even God Himself."[2]

I'm learning more each day, for our intimacy and our humility to be pure they must walk hand in hand. God desires a perfect harmony of love and discipline.

Submission is *not* the burden many think it to be. It's also *not* meant to take away your joy. Since creation, Satan has tried to deceive us into believing we'll miss out on something good when we obey God; that obedience somehow limits our happiness. But Truth is just the opposite!

Obedience to God is the most joyful, secure place you can be.

In the next few essays we're going to explore God's heart about obedience and how it opens wide the door for His Kingdom to come on earth. Come expectant. Come open to the Holy Spirit's teaching.

Come knowing the more you understand about obedience, the more you will believe:

> "It will be my joy to say, 'Your will, Your way – always'." Chris Tomlin, *Lay Me Down*

Changing Your Perspective
on Obedience
(part 2)

"Anyone who listens to My teaching and follows it is wise,
like a person who builds a house on solid rock."
Matthew 7:24 (NLT)

One of the surest signs of maturity is the ease with which you obey the Holy Spirit's leading.

As a parent or leader, you know when you give specific instructions it's for a very specific reason. You see ahead to a goal, knowing this step is part of a bigger picture and your directions are for the good of both the individual and the whole.

In the same way, the Holy Spirit desires to guide and teach you, but with purity and insight far exceeding human logic and reasoning. With impeccable wisdom, power, and love He brings together countless details over many lifetimes in just the perfect timing for a moment in your day. It's really breath-taking when you sit back and think about it.

Yet, instead of embracing His heavenly perspective, we too often sound like the toddler who constantly questions his mother's instructions.

- "Why do You want to do that?"
- "Why do You want to do it that way?"
- "Are You *sure*?"
- "Can we do it this way instead?"

When you are more aware of your physical condition than God's majesty, it's difficult to understand His ways. But with every step of obedience His sovereignty and wisdom become more and more apparent. Soon you'll ask less questions as you come to know:

Obedience is always for a purpose.

God's instructions are never pointless or cruel. Ever. They may not make immediate sense and may lead to uncomfortable or unfamiliar territory, but the Holy Spirit always leads you into truth. Obedience to His leading always takes you closer to your Creator and deeper into your divine destiny. Always.

One of my favorite examples of this is found in Peter.

Luke 5:1-11 records an encounter between Jesus and Peter early in their relationship. Peter had just finished a night of fishing and was cleaning his nets as Jesus began teaching at the Sea of Galilee. When the crowd pressed in against Him, Jesus asked to use Peter's boat to teach from.

After Jesus finished teaching, He made a very unusual request. He told Peter to put out into the deep water and lower his nets again. Peter replied,

> "Master, we toiled all night [exhaustingly] and caught nothing [in our nets]. But on the ground of Your word I will lower the nets [again]." Luke 5:5 (AMP)

When Peter obeyed Jesus' instructions, he caught such a haul of fish his nets began to break. Calling for his friends, they filled two boats so that they almost sank.

> "But when Simon Peter saw this, he fell down at Jesus' knees, saying, 'Depart from me, for I am a sinful man, O Lord'." Luke 5:8 (AMP)

I see several important lessons in this encounter:

- Obedience opens wide the door for God to use the foolish things to confound the wise.

Peter knew fishing in the middle of the day was foolish. Yet on the authority of Jesus' word, the illogical became a platform to display God's glory. If you are willing to step out on God's word, He will do more through you than you could think or imagine – often in very unusual ways.

- Obedience leads you deeper into the fear of God.

Peter had just begun his journey into knowing Jesus. Although he'd heard profound teaching and witnessed his mother-in-law's healing, this experience produced even greater reverence. The more you encounter God, the more you know He is worthy of your obedience.

- Obedience opens your eyes to see yourself in the light of God.

Even though the massive catch of fish was a physical blessing, Peter was more aware of the spiritual condition of his own heart: "*I am a sinful man.*" He recognized what was of eternal value. Seeing yourself in the light of Truth brings clarity, freedom, and growth.

- Obedience opens your understanding to a greater purpose and destiny.

Luke 5:11 tells us Peter, James, and John immediately dropped everything to follow Jesus. When you catch a glimpse of your Creator you realize life is much more than what your physical eyes can see. Earthly cares fade in the light of eternal destiny. Each single step of obedience leads to greater levels of obedience.

Catching fish wasn't the goal for Jesus that day. Peter thought it was, but in his simple step of obedience Peter found himself on the threshold of the real goal. A deeper revelation of Jesus propelled him into a legacy of catching men that continues to this day. When you allow the Holy Spirit to lead your steps, He will cause your life to reverberate throughout the ages.

What is God asking of you today?

May grace and faith rise up and empower you to step forward in obedience. May you see new aspects of God, grounding you deeper in His love and majesty. May you come to know even more that He is for you, not against you. His every command carries a purpose and destiny beyond this world.

Changing Your Perspective
on Obedience
(part 3)

"...You have given me
the capacity to hear *and* obey...

I delight to do Your will, O my God..."
Psalm 40:6, 8 (AMP)

The more I walk in obedience, the more I realize the richness of joy it brings.

Not fickle, temporary happiness, but deep down, rock-solid, pure, permeating joy.

Most of us know that obeying God is the *right* thing to do, but to equate it with *joy* can be quite a leap. We don't want to be controlled. We don't like being limited or restrained or told what to do. We fear looking like a fool or a failure.

But what if God is leading you to a destiny beyond yourself?

- What if He wants to fill you with His wisdom and passion?
- What if He wants to show you His design for Life?
- What if He wants to lead you to freedom and peace?
- To partner with you and entrust you with His mysteries?
- What if God won't let you settle for less than all He knows you can be?

To move from an earthly mindset that makes us bristle at the thought of submission to a joyful expectation of good, we must focus on the One who is leading. We must look at the full spectrum of His love, grace, and wisdom.

When God asks anything of you it's only for your good. Everything the Holy Spirit directs you to do ultimately leads to Life.

As we talked about in part 2, obedience always has a purpose. It always leads you closer to Jesus, closer to your destiny, and deeper into His Kingdom. All of this produces a divine, unshakable joy.

Jesus told His disciples in John 15:10-11 (NIV):

> "If you keep my commands, you will remain in my love, just as I have kept my Father's commands and remain in his love.
>
> I have told you this so that my joy may be in you and that your joy may be complete."

Your Creator *wants* you to be firmly rooted in His love. He *wants* you to have complete joy, not fluctuating emotions. But to find the joy of obedience, you must embrace the glory of humility. You must come to see the privilege of being led by One who is perfect in all ways.

Personally, I find it astounding that we can live in the counsel of God. And if we obey it, He trusts us as a friend. Perfect joy flourishes in this communion. (See John 15:14-15.)

Sometimes obedience takes you where you already long to go. Other times it comes in the form of small, seemingly insignificant requests, barely costing you a thing yet revealing a bigger picture.

Still other times it'll cost you more than you can imagine – your very thoughts, opinions, desires, relationships, and life. Obeying God's word can be the hardest thing you've ever experienced – but only for the moment and for a reward far greater than the price.

Look at the life of Jesus. He did nothing, He said nothing, except what the Father instructed and this obedience led Him to the cross. Painful. Lonely. Death. Yet for the *joy* set before Him Jesus endured the cross and its shame.

A reward of power, fame, or fortune didn't carry Jesus through. Neither anger nor bitterness drove Him forward. Jesus overcame the cross by knowing the pure joy of obedient trust.

Jesus understood obedience. He submitted Himself wholly to His Father's word knowing it is the most perfect place. The security of His Father's love overshadowed His pain. The reward of fulfilling His destiny eclipsed His momentary trial. The Life of God within empowered Him to be victorious.

This depth of joy only comes in the fire of obedience.

This depth of joy is what you are called to:

- being one with your God;
- abiding in His love;
- becoming His friend;
- watching His Life flow through you;
- partnering to build His Kingdom.

Each small step builds upon another until you know your God is truly worthy of your allegiance. As you believe He is all powerful, all wise, and all good it will be your joy to obey Him. It will be your joy to say:

> *Your Kingdom come, God. Your will and purpose be done. Whatever You ask, whatever You desire, I'm following You.*

Changing Your Perspective
on Obedience
(part 4)

"He said to them,
Why are you so timid *and* fearful?
How is it that you have no faith
(no firmly relying trust)?"
Mark 4:40 (AMP)

What are you afraid of? What do you stop short of, or even run from, because of hidden anxiety?

Nearly everyone, it seems, has resigned themselves in one degree or another to living with fear.

- Fear of death
- heights
- loneliness
- crowds
- change
- failure
- success
- flying
- growing old
- being poor
- getting sick
- having an accident
- meeting new people
- losing a loved one – the list is endless.

But fear isn't a quiet pet living in a cage in the back room. As termites undermine the internal workings of a structure until it collapses from within, fear spreads to every part of your life unless you deal with it.

I grew up with my own vast array of trepidations. Some were simple and childish. Others paralyzed me. I was mostly quiet; happy to blend into the wallpaper. Even when I found myself playing piano and singing in front of a crowd, I happily melted into the back corner of the group.

I was horribly claustrophobic, frightened to have anything covering my face (even water in the shower) and several times bolted from the dentist's chair when I could no longer take the tubes, lights, and hands so close.

I was scared to fly, scared to be a passenger in heavy traffic, scared of making a mistake, scared of being in the spotlight. Yep – *fear is a no-win situation.*

So how has God dealt with my fear?

The same way He dealt with Job's: By letting it come upon me in wave after wave so it could no longer hide in the dark corners of my thoughts. Then, when all seemed a loss and more than I could take, God stepped forward in beauty and power to give me a more accurate perspective.

One by one the Holy Spirit replaced my fears with love and truth. One by one I saw them as tiny grains of sand, not the mountains I'd thought.

I now see God is greater than anything fear can throw at me – and *He lives in me.*

What does this have to do with obeying God?

Think for a minute. How often does fear keep you from going deeper in your walk with Jesus? How often do you hold back from drawing closer to Him because you're afraid of what He might ask you to do?

- How many dreams lie in the back of the closet?
- How many bridges detoured around?
- How many Holy Spirit nudges ignored?

Fear will always keep you from fulfilling your destiny in Christ.

God knows this. And so – at the perfect time – He will lead you to face your fear. Not to scare you, but that you might be free. You *are* more than a conqueror through Christ Jesus, but often don't realize it until you need to.

Look at the disciples in Mark 4:35-41. They had just heard Jesus teach profound truths. They had just been told that they, of all the people, had been entrusted with the mysteries of the kingdom of God. They probably felt pretty excited about their future.

Then Jesus made a simple request: *"Let's cross to the other side of the lake."*

It seemed like a simple request, but the disciples soon found themselves in an unexpected storm. A storm of hurricane proportions. In great fear they cried out to Jesus, "Master, do You not care that we are perishing?"

The bottom line:

> You will have to face your fear if you want to follow Jesus.

You will have to face storms and obstacles. But look again at Mark 4. Where was Jesus? Sleeping in the stern of the boat. *Sleeping in the midst of the storm.*

Jesus never shines light on your fear without also revealing His peace and His power.

> "When Jesus woke up, He rebuked the wind and said to the waves, 'Silence! Be still!' Suddenly the wind stopped, and there was a great calm." (v. 39, NLT)

Obedience to God is the *safest* place you can be. Truly. There is no greater security than knowing you're in the care of a perfect, loving, powerful Creator. His wisdom surpasses all thought and His desire to see you live a life of peace and joy exceeds all imagination.

Grab onto Him. Grab onto His Word. Follow this One who is leading you to fullness of Life. And if you find you have somehow let go, know He never lets go of you.

> "I said to the man who stood at the gate of the year, 'Give me a light that I may tread safely into the unknown.'
>
> And he replied, 'Go into the darkness and put your hand into the hand of God. That shall be to you better than light and safer than a known way!'" Minnie Louise Haskins[3]

Communion in the Flames

"From what appeared to be His waist up,
He looked like gleaming amber,
flickering like a fire.

And from His waist down,
He looked like a burning flame,
shining with splendor.

All around Him was a glowing halo,
like a rainbow shining in the clouds on a rainy day.

This is what the glory of the Lord looked like to me.
When I saw it, I fell face down on the ground..."
Ezekiel 1:27-28 (NLT)

It's an amazing relationship, this communion in the flames.

While warming myself in front of the open wood stove this morning, I noticed tiny pieces of ash dancing on top of the stove. It seemed they were drawn to the edge, wanting to dive off and return to the flames. But just as they dropped off, the heat waves caused the ash to swirl up and land back on top of the stove.

I watched this mini-drama play out over and over in just a few seconds.

I wondered: *Is this a picture of living at the altar of communion?*

We are drawn by an undeniable force, closer and closer to our Creator-God. The flame of His love and glory pulls us in as we bask in His warmth.

But at an invisible edge between soul and spirit, the intensity of His fire seems to blow us back at the revelation of His purity and majesty. Over and over, drawn closer yet overwhelmed by His presence.

In recent years the Body of Christ has come through a season emphasizing the Father's love. This has been a powerful move of the Holy Spirit, bringing significant healing to many and paving the way to living lives of true worship. I love nothing more than sitting at my Father's feet.

But in basking in the love and kindness of our God, I also sense a caution: We must never forget or minimize His holiness. Our God is also a consuming fire.

If we aren't careful, we will diminish Him down to our level instead of rising to His.

Our sovereign, all-powerful Creator is not a tyrant, but neither is He a pushover. Jehovah draws us to Himself with the same intensity of love that drove Him to the cross, yet His radiating fire of holiness consumes in us all that is not pure.

If we find ourselves feeling only goose bumps of love but never the fear of God and the sting of purification we might make sure the coals within are still burning hot.

Both love *and* holiness reveal the heart of our God.

Father, Holy God, draw us closer. Pull us into Yourself – again and again and again. And may we never be the same. Refine us, oh Fire of Love, Fire of Holiness. Purify our hearts and minds. Then kiss us again. We want all of You.

Core Desire

"This is eternal life,
that they may know You, the only true God,
and Jesus Christ whom You have sent."
John 17:3 (NASB)

Our black lab, Ruby, has more personality than any dog I've known.

- She absolutely loves company, be it human or canine.
- She *always* acts like it's her birthday.
- She rarely has a foot on the ground as she hops and leaps and pounces and spins her way through the day.
- She loves life.
- And she absolutely loves the river.

I've been taking her on my morning walks more lately. Although it can be a bit distracting for my prayer time, it seems the Spirit often uses her as an object lesson. One thing I can't help but notice is how she acts every time we start in the direction of the river.

She gets more and more attentive. Then, when I let her off of the leash at the bridge, she stops every 5-10 yards to stick her head under the bottom rail to get a quick look at the water below. *It has her full focus.*

Three times this summer Ruby has disappeared. Each time we received a phone call: She'd gone to the river. Twice she swam over a mile beside a boat or tube until the fishermen pulled over at a campground and called the sheriff to come pick her up.

Her only thought was to be in the water, and preferably with company.

I love this picture. God undoubtedly made her with a core desire to swim and she has discovered it. She loves to fetch and play and explore, but it's all better in the water. She found her passion.

It then begs the question: What core desire did God put in us as humans, and have you discovered it?

I guess our talents, giftings, and activities pursued could be a part of our core desire. I've a deep love for music and writing, people and traveling, walking and exploring. And yet, I don't think any of these are my foundational passion. I believe they are simply avenues to express and explore my true core desire.

The one desire our Creator put in each and every one of us is to know Him.

Not to know *about* Him, but to *know* Him. To make memories with Him. To spend time talking together and living together and sharing the activities we love.

I almost always talk to God as I'm cooking, asking what ingredients to add or how long to cook something. (He is an *amazing* cook! Just ask my kids.) I love to tell Him how much I'm enjoying the landscape or the song I'm writing or a friendship I've made.

I know my God sees and knows all things even before they happen, but that's not the point.

The point is He wants to spend time together.

He wants us to learn how He thinks, to recognize the sound of His voice, and to see what we would've missed without Him. He wants to share with us His wisdom and creativity.

He also wants to bring the words of the Bible to life in our very own lives – for us to know what love and grace and faith and hope *really* look like when we live them out deeper each day.

This isn't always an easy process, this getting to know God. Sometimes we make mistakes when we're learning to hear His voice. Sometimes we misunderstand what He says. Sometimes we let our emotions and own ideas get mixed in and He has to bring us back to the truth – usually through the Word.

But this doesn't frustrate Him in the least. Just as loving parents get excited to see their children learning to talk and walk, so is God with us. I believe He laughs and rejoices over each attempt made, each lesson learned. I *know* His grace covers countless mishaps.

As long as we stay soft and teachable before Him, there's no limit to the places He will take us into Himself.

When Jesus prayed for us to be one with the Father even as He is, it wasn't just wishful thinking. God has been arranging for all of time to bring you to this place, today, to know Him as Creator and Father and Friend.

To know Him in the most intimate and majestic ways possible – *this* is what keeps nagging at you from your core. *This* is what you were created to do. Believe me, it will make everything else in your life come alive.

Deep to Deep

"Then he added,
"Son of man, let all my words
sink deep into your own heart first.
Listen to them carefully for yourself."
Ezekiel 3:10 (NLT)

Lord, here I am, my heart is open wide
I'm choosing now Your love instead of my pride
    Come meet with me
    Come meet with me

Your thoughts are so high – Your ways are so deep
Renew my mind and change the way I see
    Come meet with me
    Come meet with me

Pour out all You want to give
I know now, without it I can't live
Another day

Love me Lord – like You want to do
So I can do – what You ask me to

Deep to deep – pour out on me
Deep to deep – I receive
Deep to deep – Your love for me

Ears to Hear, Eyes to See

"Ears to hear and eyes to see –
both are gifts from the Lord."
Proverbs 20:12 (NLT)

There's nothing quite like having pieces of a puzzle come into order.

When we see, when we hear clearly, when we understand the significance of a word or touch from God, our lives are forever changed.

On the first day of this year, the Holy Spirit used a seemingly minor incident to allow me a fresh glimpse of His acute awareness of my every breath. In my journal I wrote,

> "Father, You did something so very profound today. It left me undone – again. It may seem silly to many who would read this, but we both know the vast and unmistakable significance."

A number of years before, I had received a sweater in a box of hand-me-downs. It had a tall neck with a full-length zipper; perfect for cool Wyoming days. I love unexpected treasures and wore it often.

Several years later, in a brief moment of idle curiosity, I opened the zipper from the bottom up. It had been made with this option, but for some reason the zipper got off track.

I tried and tried to get it back on track, or at least undone, but never could. Because it was one of my favorites, I couldn't bring myself to throw it out. I kept it in my closet but rarely wore it.

Periodically I'd get it out and try again to fix the zipper, but without success.

The first day of this year fell on a Sunday and the Spirit prompted me to wear the sweater to church. Afterwards I tried like so many times before to get the zipper undone. As I walked by my husband, Matt, I mentioned my desire and he started to work on it as well.

All along I had been pulling the same side of the zipper out of the way while working the tab, but Matt pulled the opposite side. Within seconds the sweater was hanging open.

I was stunned as the Holy Spirit opened my eyes to see much more than a zipper.

At the same time as the zipper had gotten off track, years before, so had several important relationships in my life. A seemingly small choice had taken us all in a different direction than planned, bringing friction with no apparent fix. In those circumstances, just as with the sweater, God used Matt to push to the side what was off-track, causing it all to fall apart but work as it was originally intended.

My eyes filled with tears as I saw anew my Father's perfect sovereignty.

Jesus longs for us to know Him intimately. He wants us to hear His constant whisper and glimpse His majesty. He desires to show us the mysteries and secrets of His Kingdom.

If you humble yourself before Him, God will give you the gift of seeing what only He sees; of hearing and understanding His Spirit. He will pour out wisdom in abundance, show you beauty beyond comprehension, and unleash power from realms above.

He will unfold His Word and His heart, piece by piece, as you are able to receive.

Grab a hold of Proverbs 20:12. Ask for eyes to see and ears to hear. What more could you desire than to see and know this One so perfect.

"[For I always pray to] the God of our Lord Jesus Christ, the Father of glory, that He may grant you a spirit of wisdom and revelation [of insight into the mysteries and secrets] in the [deep and intimate] knowledge of Him,

By having the eyes of your heart flooded with light, so that you can know *and* understand the hope to which He has called you..." Ephesians 1:17-18 (AMP)

Embracing the Season

"For everything there is a season,
a time for every activity under heaven."
Ecclesiastes 3:1 (NLT)

Nature teaches us so many valuable lessons. It's no wonder God often chooses the mountains or wilderness as a training ground.

I walk most every day and rarely do I come home empty-handed. Sometimes I collect thoughts that later become songs or journal entries. Other days I gather pebbles, twigs, or flowers as souvenirs to remind me years later of truths learned in His presence.

It's interesting: Even those of us who anticipate change, who get excited to see what's coming around the corner, have a tendency to hold on to the past to some degree. While collecting treasures as we travel through life is healthy, trouble comes when we cling to the past and lose step with the future.

I recently experienced an example of this with gardening.

I have an incurable love of flower gardens. I can't wait to see tulips peeking through the snow or ants toiling to help peonies open their buds. My favorite intoxication comes while standing near a lilac bush in full bloom and just a glimpse of Forget-me-nots hiding under sagebrush takes my breath.

Unfortunately, my love for flowers sometimes pushes away better judgment. Almost every fall I talk myself out of cleaning the beds, believing the sight of dead flowers poking up through the snow will remind me new life is sure to come.

While this gives a measure of joy, it mostly makes for a more difficult job in the spring.

A few days ago I finally pruned back last year's leftovers from my rapidly growing plants. As I labored on my knees, two details struck me.

- First, there was no way to get all of the dead branches and leaves out of my thriving plants. No matter how hard I tried, some brown stalks remained.

- Second, I damaged the new growth in my efforts to clean out what should've been pruned months before.

In holding onto the pleasure of last summer, I failed to recognize the beauty and purpose of a clean flower bed hiding beneath the snow.

Isn't that the way with life? Each season holds its purpose. Some flourish with growth. Others are meant for rest. When we try to overlap the two we often steal from the past and damage what's to come.

I've been blessed to be involved in fruitful ministry where I experienced my Father's pleasure. But at times I've held on to successes of the past when the Spirit was leading in a new direction. As a result, fragments of my heart longed for what had been instead of resting and preparing for what was to come.

Then, when the Holy Spirit led me to new assignments, I had to cut out distractions that now impeded fresh growth.

- At times I've held too tightly to friends when God wanted to take them in another direction to build new relationships and fulfill destinies.
- Music that ministered in the last season but wasn't for today filled my mind when the Spirit wanted to give new songs.

- Activities resonating with God's presence yesterday now seemed hollow.

Sadly, I had allowed remnants of the last season to stay too long and new growth was damaged while pruning them out.

"For everything there is a season, a time for every activity under heaven." What an essential truth. We don't despise yesterday if we embrace tomorrow. We're simply honoring what God desires for each individual season. In this way we honor Him.

Do you recognize the season you're in?
How do you keep in step with the Holy Spirit?

Fire of Love

"The angel of the Lord appeared to him
in a blazing fire from the midst of a bush;

and he looked, and behold,
the bush was burning with fire,
yet the bush was not consumed."
Exodus 3:2 (NASB)

Fire from above, come down
Fire from above, consume
Fire from above, come down
Consume in me, oh Lord, with love

All of what I have, I give
All of who I am, I leave
All of what I do, no more
Consume in me, oh Lord, with love

> Burn away, burn away
> Burn away me
> Burn away, burn away
> Burn away me

Only You, my God, in me
Only You, my King, I see
Only You, my God, in me
Consume in me, oh Lord, with love

Burn away, burn away
Burn away me
Burn away, burn away
Burn away me

Let the fire of Your love consume me, Lord
Let the fire of Your love consume me, Lord
Let the fire of Your love consume me, Lord

Again and again
Again and again and again

"For Me"

> "But I will raise up for Myself
> a faithful priest who will do
> according to what is in
> My heart and in My soul;
> and I will build him an enduring house,
> and he will walk before My anointed always."
> I Samuel 2:35 (NASB)

You know those days when you ask: *"Why am I doing this?"*

Those days when:

- the task seems bigger than it did yesterday.
- the goal seems a bit fuzzy.
- energy is waning and you just want to sit down.

I had one of those days last week. I was tired – mentally, physically, emotionally tired.

This year has been a "Go forward" year. I've been moving out of comfort zones and into new territory with writing, music, and marketing. I *know* I'm doing what I'm supposed to do; there's been too much confirmation. But the question still caught in my throat: *"Why?"*

Warm water ran over my face as I read the white-board in the shower:

Pray.
Obey.

Rest.
Believe.
Trust.
Go forward!

I read the words several times, although they're memorized from sharing my mornings with them for the last two years. They make perfect sense. Words I believe and cling to. Yet my weary mind stepped sideways for a moment.

"Why?" I asked. *"Why am I doing this?"*

And as soft as the water on my neck, He said, *"For Me."*

Suddenly the warm water felt like oil. Warm healing balm. Strengthening marrow.

Two words. Two simple words, yet they echoed over and over in my thoughts. Even now I hear them:

"For Me."
"For Me."
"For Me."
"For Me."
"For Me."

With two words He brought me back down to the foundation. Two words wiped away all sub-points and secondary reasons. Sure, I love what I do, but I don't do it because I love it. *I do it because I love Him.* And I love Him like I never knew I could because He loves me like I never knew I could be loved.

No other reason is needed. No other cause or motivation necessary. Not when I hear His voice.

Yes, I will do it for You. I will go forward. I will expect. I will believe. I will not be disappointed. Because You are worth it all.

"Just as it is written, 'Behold, I lay in Zion a stone of stumbling and a rock of offense, And he who believes in Him will not be disappointed'." Romans 9:33 (NASB)

Fountain of Life

"...Jesus stood and He cried in a loud voice,
If any man is thirsty, let him come to Me and drink!"
John 7:37 (AMP)

I often write bible verses and quotes from books or teachings on cards and hang them around my home: precious reminders of a Father who speaks to me.

Unfortunately, when I get busy these miniature signposts start to fade into the scenery.

This morning as I hung a scrap of paper with a phone number on my cork board, I saw a note from this past year:

> "I am of the opinion that we should not be concerned about working for God until we have learned the meaning and delight of worshiping Him." A.W. Tozer, *Whatever Happened to Worship*

I literally stopped in my tracks as the words ran like warm oil over my heart and mind. "*Slow down, Amy*," they seemed to say. "*Worship*."

And I just stood there, breathing Him in.

After a while I felt compelled to walk around my home and read cards I'd too long overlooked. I'm worshiping my way through my morning, drinking again from fountains of Life; fountains connected to the one true Fountain, Jesus.

I'd like to share a few. May you be refreshed as well.

"L-O-V-E
It is a small, four-letter word that will cost you everything. Laying down your life. Passion and compassion. Giving without expecting. Feeling His very heartbeat and surrendering to His rhythm. Following the Lamb wherever He goes..." Heidi Baker, IRIS Ministries, Mozambique

"Thou hast made us for thyself, O Lord, and our heart is restless until it finds its rest in thee." Saint Augustine

"The Lord will perfect that which concerneth me: thy mercy, O Lord, endureth forever." Psalm 138:8 (KJV)

"We release through our shadow whatever overshadows us." Bill Johnson, Bethel Church

"Did I not say to you that if you would believe you would see the glory of God?" *Jesus*: John 11:40 (NASB)

"No matter the issue or conflict, the answer is more of Him!" Bill Johnson, Bethel Church

What special words have given you strength, hope, or encouragement? Pull them back out and take another drink.

Get Low

"...Under his shadow I delighted to sit,
and his fruit was sweet to my taste."
Song of Solomon 2:3 (AMP)

I just spent the last hour and a half picking raspberries, even after picking for nearly that long a few days ago.

I'm amazed at how many berries can grow on a few little bushes.

For most of the last 20 years we've been blessed to have a raspberry patch and every year I can remember the Holy Spirit has told me the same object lesson as I harvest the fruit, sometimes adding details as the years go on.

If I stand over my bushes, I see quite a few ripe berries. But not until I bend low, getting down on my knees or even sitting on the ground, do I realize the extent of the harvest.

Almost without exception, as soon as I think I've finally picked a bush clean, I turn, change my angle a little, and find a few more handfuls.

Over and over throughout the years I'm reminded of how this applies to the way we see the people around us.

Sometimes we see a little fruit here and there in the lives of others, or maybe no fruit at all, and dismiss them as "not very productive" and needing to get their act together. We may even compare our own life to theirs and think we sure have more fruit than they do.

But if we get low, if we humble ourselves before God and each other, more than likely we'll find ripe, lush berries hidden from first glances.

- Maybe gentleness concealed behind a busy schedule.
- Or strength of character lost in the leaves of a quiet personality.
- Perhaps long suffering and patience go unnoticed by those who quickly pass by.
- Maybe small but very sweet berries of willingness before the Lord are obscured by misunderstandings.

Taking this humble position is more important than we often realize. Our pride can cause us to miss the opportunity to feast on the goodness of God growing all around us. Just as the fruit on a raspberry bush is meant to be eaten, the spiritual fruit in the people around us is meant to be consumed to gain much needed spiritual nourishment.

If we look at another person from the position of pride, we may miss the very provision of God's grace, love, or wisdom we need for this day.

Only in humility will we see through the eyes of our Father and recognize His working in and through those around us. Only in humility will we be able to partake of His goodness in them, and in turn have fruit in our own lives to nourish others.

> "You will show me the path of life; in Your presence is fullness of joy, at Your right hand there are pleasures forevermore." Psalm 16:11 (AMP)

Go Ahead – Receive it!

"Whoever receives His testimony
has set his seal of approval to this:
God is true.

[That man has definitely certified, acknowledged,
declared once and for all, and is himself assured
that it is divine truth that God cannot lie.]"
John 3:33 (AMP)

It was another crisp, clear day in Jackson Hole.

Snow-covered mountains swam in cerulean skis. Brilliant sunshine beckoned even the laziest of us away from the fireplace and into subzero temperatures to soak up a bit of its energy. So, after numerous chores and duties, I found myself crunching down the bike path, praying under my breath as I studied the horizon.

I knew I would be coming into town to do some writing, but wasn't sure yet of the topic or direction. As I walked, I asked, "Father, what do You want me to write about?"

And in that perfect, priceless way, He whispered back, "*Me.*"

I couldn't help myself: I giggled. I just can't get over it. How can this all-powerful Almighty One be so gentle and humorous? And how can He be so specific and yet so *not* specific?

Consequently, there I sat in my favorite coffee shop, wondering which one of His many attributes I should write about. I opened my bible and landed on page 1212. As I scanned the very familiar page, I was drawn to a verse I've been led to many, many times – John 3:33 (above).

Although this particular verse may not jump up and melt your heart, I believe it's like a hinge on a door. It holds truth on which much, if not all, of our future depends.

John 3:33 is a pivotal point in our destiny.

John the Baptist is speaking here to his disciples. It comes near the end of a conversation when they'd come to John concerned so many were now following Jesus instead of him.

Very quickly John clarifies, again, he is not the Messiah but only a messenger called to prepare the way for Jesus. He then gives some very important insight into our own heart posture for following Christ.

First, John says, "Whoever receives His testimony..."

You know, most of us live in a world where we've lost touch with the force of what *receiving* really means.

- We're given gifts from friends and family, but put them in a closet to gather dust.
- We buy food, but allow it to spoil in the fridge before we have time to eat it.
- We acknowledge the opinions and beliefs of others without ever taking time to dig to the bottom of the matter and form our own foundation of belief.

Contrast this half-heartedness to the Greek meaning of *lambanō,* translated in John 3:33 as *receives:*

> *"to take with the hand, lay hold of in order to use it; to take in order to carry away; to take to one's self, to make one's own; that which when taken is not let go, to seize, to lay hold of, apprehend; take possession of, i.e. to appropriate to one's self; reach after, strive to obtain."*[5]

This receiving of Jesus' testimony John speaks of is not an indifferent reaction. When we *receive* the words and teachings of Jesus, we grab ahold of them and make them our very own.

- We tear open the outside packaging and inspect every sheet of tissue paper so we don't miss any piece or part.
- We hold it in our hands, slowly turning it over and around to study each detail.
- We keep this gift with us at all times, allowing it to alter who we are and what we do.
- We continually draw from its Life while offering it to others.
- We do this until we can't imagine not doing it.

This is receiving the testimony of Jesus.

When we take these conscious, fixed, continual steps of receiving, the second half of John 3:33 tells us the result: *We set our seal of approval to this: God is true.*

Or as the Amplified Bible states it, we acknowledge, declare, and are assured that "*God cannot lie.*"

Literally, the Greek word *alēthēs*[6] here means we know without wavering God loves the truth, speaks the truth, and is truthful.

Yes, I know we *say* God would never lie, but imagine what you'd look like and act like if you believed to your very core every one of the thousands of promises and statements of God to be true.

Imagine what the Body of Christ would look like.

Talk about peace. Talk about humility and love and joy. If we believed all God has spoken is true, nothing could shake us. Nothing could cause us to waver. Nothing would be worth holding onto when He asks it from us. Nothing. We would agree with His desires and plans implicitly, even if it hurt, because we knew His truth of love and faithfulness wouldn't fail under even the gravest of circumstances.

We would believe that to live is Christ and to die is gain. (See Philippines 1:21.)

How do we get to this unshakable place of rest the writer of Hebrews exhorts us to zealously pursue? (See Hebrews 4:11.) Receive. Receive the testimony of Jesus.

Go back and read His words. Open them up, piece by piece. And don't just read the words, but let the Holy Spirit read them to you. Let Him shine holy, heavenly Light on them to give you understanding. Then hold them close; close enough to burn into your soul.

I find myself smiling, again, as I realize this process of receiving is a bit like my Father's answer to me as I walked: so specific and yet so not specific. That's ok. He knows how vast He is. Just take a step up to the door and He will meet you and do all that you can't.

Believe me, it's worth it!

God, the Builder

"For [of course] every house
is built *and* furnished by someone,

but the Builder of all things
and the Furnisher
[of the entire equipment of all things]
is God."
Hebrews 3:4 (AMP)

Building a home excites me.

From wish lists to the smell of cut lumber to filling kitchen cupboards, I enjoy every stage of construction. It speaks of new beginnings, fresh vision, and team work.

Matt and I have built two homes in the last 24 years. Both took all of our time, energy, and resources. Both drew us to physical and emotional limits, yet fed a core need to create.

Through long nights and tired muscles, cracked fingers and eating peanut butter and bread for days, we treasured both the process and the end result.

As I read Hebrews 3:4 (above), I smile thinking of God this way:

God – the Builder.
God – the Furnisher.

What passion must flow from divine depths as vision takes form. As destiny and reality meet. I can imagine the fire singing in Jesus' eyes even as a grin graces His lips:

Bringing parts and pieces together from around the globe. Building what no man could think or imagine.

Look around. Not with physical eyes only, but spiritual.

- What is the great Builder building in you?
- In those around you?
- In your family, community, and nation?
- How is He furnishing these humble, glorious homes with Himself and heaven?

Can you hear the hammers and chisels at work? Can you see the siding going up and the windows being set?

God is building His Church, His Bride, His dwelling place, His Kingdom.

The process may press you to your limits. It may stretch your thinking and stamina. It may bring up questions you hadn't thought of and reveal steps you didn't foresee.

But know this: You are not a mistake or afterthought. When the Creator of the universe builds and furnishes, He does it with all the love and wisdom of the ages.

You – His Church, His Bride, His dwelling place – you are masterfully designed, precisely engineered, and perfectly fashioned. You are beautiful!

Embrace the season, with all of its long nights and worn knees. It's worth it!

> "O afflicted one, storm-tossed, *and* not comforted, Behold, I will set your stones in antimony, And your foundations I will lay in sapphires.
>
> Moreover, I will make your battlements of rubies, And your gates of crystal, And your entire wall of precious stones." Isaiah 54:11-12 (NASB)

Grace to See Me Through

"For the word of the Lord holds true,
and we can trust everything he does."
Psalm 33:4 (NLT)

So many people I know and care for are going through very trying times – physically, financially, emotionally, and spiritually.

Everything in our families, marriages, relationships, health, and work that can be stretched, tested, and tried seems to be getting the full force in recent years. I know the consuming, refining fire of God has touched my own life on many levels, burning away what brought death, purifying what brings life, and strengthening my faith in the process.

Many questions arise in the midst of difficult hours.

- God, where are You?
- Why aren't my prayers being answered?
- Why aren't miracles happening in my life?

My thought is this: Which is the greater miracle, a sudden and complete change in our circumstances or a grace that sees us through when the change comes over a long journey?

Is an immediate healing a greater miracle than the joy one discovers as they hide deep in God's love and peace while still in pain? Does greater faith come from a quick release from addiction as opposed to a daily walking out the truth of the Word until you know you are no longer bound in sin and shame?

Although our God still performs instantaneous or sudden miracles, I'm not so sure faster is *always* greater in His eyes.

Think of our Creator's declaration to Paul in the midst of his pain and torment:

> "My grace (My favor and loving-kindness and mercy) is enough for you [sufficient against any danger and enables you to bear the trouble manfully]; for *My* strength *and* power are made perfect (fulfilled and completed*) and show themselves most effective* in [your] weakness..." II Corinthians 12:9 (AMP)

This new understanding caused Paul to then declare:

> "Therefore, I will all the more gladly glory in my weaknesses *and* infirmities, that the strength *and* power of Christ (the Messiah) may rest (yes, may pitch a tent over and dwell) upon me!"

David gives us another great example of the value of perseverance in painful circumstances. Many of the psalms contain his cries of anguish and distraught, but end in a firm declaration of trust and devotion.

God knew what path would best lead to David's maturity in faith and wisdom, allowing David to learn the reality of the hidden place during the refining process.

God knows just as perfectly what path will bring the chaff to the surface in your life so you gain freedom and He can move without restriction through you.

I've had many days when my heart lay broken and my hope crushed. I couldn't see a way through the darkness and couldn't imagine a time of joy ahead.

And yet, the power of God's Word would gird and strengthen me as I resolved to cling to its truths. The wind of the Spirit would blow on my face and refresh me when I didn't think I could go on.

And as I humbled myself before my Maker, believing His plan was still somehow perfect, grace would overflow to me and bring peace and joy in the midst of unanswered questions.

Freedom and healing came as I experienced the endless supply of Christ in me. This is indeed a great miracle.

I don't know where you're walking right now or what you may be going through, but God's love is the same to each and every one of us. His plans are always perfect and His ways full of power and wisdom.

If you find yourself stepping from sickness to healing or debt to riches in one movement, rejoice and press yet deeper into your Father's goodness and presence.

If, however, you are on a longer journey with the hope still before you, know without wavering or doubt: Each step still contains a miracle – a miracle of love, a miracle of grace, a miracle of peace, a miracle of freedom – as you lean on Him and rest in His truth.

Greater Than Our Frailty

"Sing to the Lord with thanksgiving;
Sing praises to our God on the lyre,

Who covers the heavens with clouds,
Who provides rain for the earth,
Who makes grass to grow on the mountains."
Psalm 147:7-8 (NASB)

I've heard a number of my Christian friends say recently, "Life is so fragile."

And though I agree life is neither predictable nor easy, something deep within me wants to say, *"But our God is so much greater than our frailty!"*

- Not a hair falls from your head that He doesn't see.
- Not a word from your mouth that He didn't already know about at the beginning of time.
- He is aware of your need before you ask and has – for centuries – worked to bring intricate details together for your destiny.

You are the object of His undying affection.

I'm not ignoring our limitations as human beings, in and of ourselves. But with all of the chaos, all of the danger, all of the mess mankind has made, our God is still completely aware, perfect in power, passionately in love, and forever on time.

No issue confounds Him, no power eclipses Him, and all pure love finds its source in Him.

With all of the beauty and majesty in the universe, *we* are His most prized creation. He has moved mountains, calmed seas, and given His life for us. He offers us shelter in the shadow of His wing and invites us to live eternal in the fortress of His faithfulness.

I think back to foolish things I've done – hanging out with the wrong people at the wrong time; driving way too fast or through blinding snowstorms; walking down dark alleys and riding deserted subways alone – and I wonder how I've survived as long as I have.

Yet this I know:

- It is my God who laid the foundations of the earth and determined its dimensions.
- It is my Savior who, with a word, set the boundaries of the sea and knows where the gates of death exist.
- It is our Creator who provides food for the ravens when their young cry out in hunger and makes daylight spread to the ends of the earth to bring an end to the night's wickedness.

Why would we think we're not under His constant watch-care?

Mankind is compared to grass numerous times in the Word, but this isn't so much about frailty as to remind us that our lives are fleeting. Our time on this earth is but a breath in the bigger picture of eternity. Our physical bodies are temporary, while God is eternal.

Unexpected events can happen in a moment and life can be changed in a heartbeat. We can get sick or lose a loved one without having seen a warning sign. But these sudden changes were only unexpected to *us*. The One who created us is neither surprised nor apathetic.

God is more active than we could ever imagine keeping us alive, safe, full of hope, and growing.

Yes, you should treasure each breath as a gift and not take a moment for granted. But you're not called to live out your life in fear of what tomorrow holds.

You aren't just floating around in space, prey to random disaster and chance attack.

Jesus assures us in John 10:28-29 (AMP):

> "...no one is able snatch (you) out of My hand. My Father, Who has given (you) to Me, is greater and mightier than all [else]..."

And if you don't know Jesus yet, if you haven't given Him control of your heart, still you're under His loving-care more than you realize:

> "For He gives His sunlight to both the evil and the good, and He sends rain on the just and the unjust alike." Matthew 5:45 (NLT)

When disaster strikes, when sickness comes, when the unexpected becomes your reality: Remember the One who holds all wisdom and releases His power on your behalf. Take comfort in His presence and let Him lead you to a Rock high above your storm.

This world may be temporal and abundant with trials, but a life hidden in Christ is not dictated by chance. Your Savior is doing much in your midst.

He Loves Like No Other

"Now, most people would not be willing
to die for an upright person,
though someone might perhaps be willing to die
for a person who is especially good.

But God showed his great love for us by sending Christ
to die for us while we were still sinners."
Romans 5:7-8 (NLT)

I've been undone again and again the last few days. It's too much to take in that the One whose words hold the universe in place would limit Himself to a human body in order for us to become one with Him.

Such love knows no bounds.

It changed death to Life. Darkness to Light. Despair to Hope.

This is not just a good story, but the only salvation for hurting, dying people. It's what drives me to continue when I don't know what my next step will be. When voices all around me are shouting, "Get out! The ship is sinking!" – even then He enables me to confidently say:

"The Lord God is my strength and my song, and He has become my salvation." Isaiah 12:2 (NASB)

This God who became a child;
this child who grew into a man;
this man who obeyed His Father and defied all darkness;
this Son who became a King.

This is the One I stand in awe of.
This is the One who makes me tremble and weep.
This is the One I wake each day to live for and hold to each night when I fall asleep.

I can't help but love this One, Jesus, for *He loves* like no other.

How Can I Deny

"May mercy and peace and love
be multiplied to you."
Jude 1:2 (NASB)

Sometimes they comes like a gentle rain
Sometimes like a hurricane
Sometimes when I least expect
Sometimes like my very next breath

Oh, how can I deny
Your tender mercies, God
They stretch from earth to sky
And wrap me up in Your great plan
A plan too great – but here I am

In Your tender mercies, God
They stretch from earth to sky
And wrap me up in Your great plan
A plan too great – oh, how can I deny!

If You Believe

"And this is what God has testified:
He has given us eternal life, and this life is in his Son."
I John 5:11 (NLT)

I'm reading an amazing book: *The Heavenly Man* by Brother Yun with Paul Hattaway.

I was drawn to it the first time I saw it, like I am to most books about Christian martyrs or the Chinese Church. I had barely read the introduction and my heart was burning.

I saw the unmistakable mark of the Life of Christ.

The opening paragraphs tell of Brother Yun being arrested in 2001 for his involvement in spreading Christianity in China; he was beaten nearly to death and sentenced to seven years in prison. A message carried out of the prison to concerned family and friends did not reflect pain or loss, however. Instead, it read:

> "God has sent me to be his witness in this place.
> There are many people here who need Jesus. I will be
> in this prison for exactly the length of time God has
> determined. I won't leave one moment early and I
> won't stay one moment too long. When God
> determines my ministry in prison is complete, I will
> come out."[7]

Only faith refined in the fire of God could answer this way.

I remember a day last fall while walking by the river. The sound of cold water and the crunch of fallen leaves spoke of the approaching winter.

As I looked up at the bare cottonwood trees, the Holy Spirit asked, *"What do you see?"*

I answered back in my mind: *Death. No, hibernation. No...*

Then, before I could go on, the Holy Spirit answered His own question: *"In season."*

I had to pause and think before the words sunk in. The stark, naked tree in front of me *looked* like death, but wasn't really dead; it was perfectly in season.

Those simple words have come back to me so many times.

Outward appearances often lead one to think circumstances are against them. John 10:10 warns us the thief's purpose is to steal, kill, and destroy.

But the second half of the verse gives us the more accurate picture when we are trusting in Truth:

> "...I came that they may have life, and have *it* abundantly." (NASB)

Jesus is Life. There is no death in Him and He has conquered death for all who believe this. Therefore, no matter the circumstances we find ourselves in, there Life will be when Christ is in us.

Brother Yun found himself bloody and bruised, but still proclaimed the Life of Christ residing within him. He knew wherever he was Jesus was with him bringing hope and joy, peace and victory.

Circumstances may look negative on the outside, but simply prove to be stepping stones for the glory of God to those who believe there is no place where Life cannot push through.

Just like a bare tree looks pretty bleak but still carries life within that will break forth in spring, our lives will also burst forth with hope and promise as we believe and trust in the purpose of each season.

May the words Jesus spoke to Martha moments before raising her brother, Lazarus, from the dead, be with us always:

> "Did I not tell you *and* promise you that if you would believe *and* rely on Me, you would see the glory of God?" John 11:40 (AMP)

If You Could Ask for Anything

> "Ask, and it will be given to you;
> seek, and you will find;
> knock, and it will be opened to you."
> Matthew 7:7 (NASB)

If you could ask for anything, what might it be?

Would you want to go on a vacation, be out of debt, win a lottery? Are you in need of basic necessities – food, water, or shelter? Would you ask for release from pain or freedom from an abusive relationship?

How about if you could ask for any character trait, what would you desire? Would you want more patience, more joy, more peace?

Right now, in your current circumstances, what one thing would you ask of your Creator-God?

It's not an easy question. We think we know what we want; we even verbalize these desires daily. But when faced with the thought of actually standing before God and asking with the expectation of receiving, many times our words fade away and our thoughts are not so clear.

For myself, I've come to realize I frequently don't know what is best. I've too often prayed and asked for one thing, but God's perfect answer was just the opposite. What I thought I wanted and needed was really not God's best in the bigger picture. I've learned His wisdom and ways are truly above and beyond logic.

Take Acts 4:29. Peter and John are gathered with other believers to pray. They had just been released from a night in prison and questioned before the rulers, elders, and leaders of the religious law in Jerusalem. They were rebuked sharply for teaching about and healing in the name of Jesus.

The council threatened Peter and John further, but finally let them go, not wanting to start a riot amongst those who were praising God for a lame man being healed.

Imagine finding yourself in Peter and John's situation. Threatened. Persecuted. Imprisoned.

How would you pray? What would you ask for? Protection? God's favor? Would you rebuke demonic attack? Would you re-think your decision to step out so publicly for Jesus?

Many years ago, while reading Acts 3-4, all of these questions went through my mind. I distinctly remember being stunned when I read verse 29: *"And now, O Lord, hear their threats, and give your servants great boldness in their preaching."*

Boldness? They asked for boldness?

I couldn't wrap my young mind around the idea of praying for the boldness to go back into a potentially painful, even deadly, situation. I remember pondering that verse over and over, wondering if I'd ever be strong enough or brave enough or convinced enough to pray that way.

Today, as I read this, I know without doubt Peter and John prayed the perfect prayer. They asked for the choicest of things. Why? Because fear, not prison or the threats of rulers, was Peter and John's greatest enemy.

Fear paralyzes. Fear breeds doubt. If they would have shrunk back the least amount, letting their imaginations be influenced by fear, fear would have then limited their ability to see, hear, and obey God.

Peter and John would go on to see amazing displays of God's wisdom and power, as well as experience great hardship and persecution. John was tortured and eventually banished to the island of Patmos. Peter was crucified upside-down. In spite of intense adversity, they never expressed regret for giving their lives for Christ's sake.

Instead, as the Holy Spirit continued to strengthen them by grace, filling them with boldness and faith, they walked out destinies we are still talking and writing about today.

As you pray, be still and let the Spirit show you *how* to pray. You may not ask for what you were planning, but God always knows perfectly what you need.

In the Light
of the King's Face

"In the light of a king's face is life,
And his favor is like a cloud with the spring rain."
Proverbs 16:15 (NASB)

There's nothing quite like sunshine.

After a week of coughing, sore throat, and overflowing sinuses, I'm so excited to be feeling better. Along with a few home remedies and a pot of really good homemade chicken-coconut soup, one of the most healing elements was sitting out in the sunshine.

Warm rays brought color back to my checks and lifted my spirit like the iris bulbs popping up in the flower beds. I love the smell of wet earth and my every pore seemed to pause and soak in the fragrance as I listened to snow melt off the roof.

But if I'm honest, it took the prodding of the Holy Spirit to get me out there.

After several days of barely doing anything, little chores kept tugging at me. Although I love watching spring unfold its wings, I found myself keeping busy even as my heart longed to go outside.

There seems to be an inherent desire in us to always be busy, doesn't there?

- Some like to work skillfully with their hands.
- Some work at developing their physical strength.
- Still others constantly expand their mental capacity.

Many stay busy, often without realizing, through endless entertainment – games, music, movies, activities, and even relationships.

While all of these can express who you are and what you enjoy, lingering in silence with your Maker, allowing His Spirit to minister deep within, accomplishes more than you can imagine.

Reading the Bible, prayer, and worship are important ingredients to our walk with Christ, but we need regular times of simply enjoying being with the One we love.

As I sat soaking in the sun, it was easy to picture myself also soaking in the Son of God. I closed my eyes until I was more aware of His Life flowing through me than even the sound of my own breath.

Sometimes in these moments He speaks, sometimes not. But with or without words, the Holy Spirit always does what I cannot – in me, for me, and afterwards, through me.

I love this reminder from Martin Smith's autobiography:

> "The sound of our songs should never drown out the silence required to listen to God. The busyness of 'doing great things for God' should never take us away from His feet."[8]

How hard is it to sit at the feet of Jesus?

To stop and bend down and quiet yourself before the One who knows the secrets of your soul, the thoughts of your mind, the desires of your heart?

How hard is it to shed pretense, ambition, and activity before the One who knows neither anxiety nor fear? To rest before the One who holds the universe in place by His word? Not His strength of action, but by a word.

Close your eyes and gaze into His. You will not find contempt here, only overflowing love, joy, and hope.

You won't always understand at the time what God is doing as you sit quietly with Him, yet later you'll notice greater strength and courage, you'll sense a softened heart, and you'll realize new revelations of His grace and mercy.

It's true; God never leaves us. David proclaimed in Psalm 139:7-10 (NIV):

> "Where can I go from your Spirit? Where can I flee from your presence? If I go up to the heavens, you are there; if I make my bed in the depths, you are there. If I rise on the wings of the dawn, if I settle on the far side of the sea, even there your hand will guide me, Your right hand will hold me fast."

Yet David also experienced an intense, deep-rooted longing to dwell in the inner courts of his King, to gaze upon God's beauty and meditate in His temple.

> "For a day in Your courts is better than a thousand [anywhere else]…" Psalm 84:10 (AMP)

Just as there's a difference between sitting in the house with sunshine coming through the window and going outside and soaking in its warmth, there's also a huge difference between knowing God is everywhere and stopping to bathe in His presence.

Take a minute. Take 30 minutes. Take a day.

Be still and lean back into the Source of Life. Let Him fill and rejuvenate you for the path ahead. It's His great desire and pleasure.

Is It Worthy?

"The temptations in your life
are no different from what others experience.
And God is faithful.

He will not allow the temptation
to be more than you can stand.
When you are tempted,
he will show you a way out so that you can endure."
I Corinthians 10:13 (NLT)

It's interesting how tightly we hold to what hurts us. How we feel justified in our fear or anger or frustration, and so cling to it even as it drains life from us.

Last night, in the last minutes of a good day, a few words were spoken. A reaction was misinterpreted. And in a moment an old feeling came to visit. It caught me off-guard, the last thing I expected, yet there I stood. Angry.

I finished my routine and crawled silently into bed. He said, I'm sorry. He did the right thing, yet something in me held to that bitter taste in my mouth. I couldn't quite let it go.

Then in the silence, a familiar verse came to mind, *"Don't let the sun go down while you are still angry, for anger gives a foothold to the devil."* Ephesians 4:26-27 (NLT)

It rang through the silence, echoing back and forth, back and forth in my thoughts. And I whispered in my mind "Lord, I don't want the sun to go down on my anger."

That's all it took. A silent whisper. A desire. An opening. And Your Light burst through. Your Word separated the darkness and gave me a way out as You asked one simple question:

"In the light of eternity,
is this anger worthy of your attention?"

In the light of eternity?

In the light of what it means to my relationship with You? In light of Your love and faithfulness? Is this anger *worthy*? Does it deserve more adoration than You?

When I'm standing before You at the end of time, do I want to be clinging to my anger?

"Of course not!" I thought.

In a split second anger was in the Light and slid from my heart's grasp. Bitterness left my mouth and heaviness ran off my mind like rainwater off a leaf. My body relaxed and I took a deep breath.

Then for a moment the tempter reminded me that I was "justified" in my feelings. But again came the firm, gentle voice: *"In light of eternity, is it worthy of your attention?"* And my spirit rose up, "No!"

Only You, Lord. Only what is pure and kind and gracious. Only what is loving and wise. Only what will come through the refining flames and cause Your smile to shine upon me. Only what brings and gives Life. Only this is worthy of my attention.

- Not anger.
- Not fear.
- Not doubt.
- Not jealousy.
- Not anxiety or frustration.
- Not anything that separates me from You.

Have you ever noticed how something that seemed *so* important suddenly loses its power when put in the proper perspective?

- Relationships you cling to, even as they kill you: When the Light of truth breaks through you see what you never saw before.

- Feelings you believe are justified, even though you've forgotten the reasons why: When Grace steps in, truth overrides emotion and you are free.

Is something you're holding to stealing your joy? Are you allowing it to simmer under the covers of justification? Look at it again.

In the light of eternity, is it worthy of your attention?

Thank You, Father, for giving a way out. Thank You for Your understanding and perspective. May it ever be before me. May I dwell always in Your presence.

Just Angry or Inspired?

"Be still before the Lord and wait patiently for him;
do not fret when men succeed in their ways,
when they carry out their wicked schemes.

Refrain from anger and turn from wrath;
do not fret – it leads only to evil.
For those who are evil will be destroyed,
but those who hope in the Lord will inherit the land."
Psalm 37:7-9 (NIV)

More and more I find myself experiencing polar-opposite emotions.

My soul is increasingly aware of and overcome by grief, even anger, at the degree of pain and injustice I see in the earth.

At the very same time, I'm more confident than ever of the perfect wisdom, goodness, and power of my Creator. I am sure of His unending faithfulness, infallible justice, and eternal plan. I witness it daily.

I know many of you have wrestled with this same paradox. We can't deny the death, greed, and untruths surrounding us. Political, social, and spiritual arenas are exploding with immorality and conflict, yet we *know* the God we serve is without fault or weakness.

So how do we bring the parts and pieces together for clear direction? Are we supposed to be doing something?

Jesus' life sheds light on our path.

John 2 records Passover was approaching so Jesus went up to Jerusalem. There He found the Temple enclosure being used as a marketplace.

This wasn't the first time Jesus had been to the Temple. This wasn't the first time He had witnessed the livestock and money changers. But He entered the courtyard with a specific purpose, unique to that day.

> "Jesus made a whip from some ropes and chased them all out of the Temple. He drove out the sheep and cattle, scattered the money changers' coins over the floor, and turned over their tables.
>
> Then, going over to the people who sold doves, he told them, 'Get these things out of here. Stop turning my Father's house into a marketplace!'" John 2:15-16 (NLT)

Yes, I think it's safe to say Jesus was angry. He didn't walk gently through the courtyard and ask everyone to please leave. He aggressively turned over tables and swung a whip to chase out the cattle and sheep.

But the next verse is key:

> "Then his disciples remembered this prophecy from the Scriptures: 'Passion for God's house will consume me'."

Jesus saw into the hearts of those who sold doves and sheep for sacrifices. He had witnessed their manipulation and greed many times and felt a righteous anger.

But His actions were not simply a reaction to anger. His actions were inspired by the heart and Word of His Father.

As we open ourselves to the words of the Bible and the presence of God we *will* be affected by them. The deeper we press into God, the more aware we will become of the darkness covering the earth.

We can respond in one of three ways.

- We can randomly lash out at the world in anger.
- We can ignore it and say everything will just work out.
- Or we can let the Word and the Spirit of God inspire us to specific action.

In this particular story, Jesus was moved by the Father to clean out the Temple courtyard. Jesus' passion for His Father's honor and His obedience to His Father's voice manifested in an aggressive demonstration of authority.

This same passion and obedience also led Jesus to walk silently to the cross.

How should we react to the upheaval around us? How should we respond to the violence and abuse? The pride, deception, and manipulation?

We can't just turn our heads. Jesus didn't. But neither can we lash out in a purely emotional rage.

- We must saturate ourselves with the Word and the presence of our Father.
- We must learn to hear His heart and instructions for each moment.
- And we must act – not out of anger, but from divine inspiration.

One moment He may tell you to boldly step forward and fight for justice. The next to quietly love the one beside you. In both, Jesus taught us to pray, "Your Kingdom come, Your will be done on earth as it is in heaven."

Only the King of kings knows how to bring His Kingdom to earth. We must ask and obey.

"Commit everything you do to the Lord. Trust him, and he will help you.

He will make your innocence radiate like the dawn, and the justice of your cause will shine like the noonday sun." Psalm 37:5-6 (NLT)

Kingdom Song

"Your people will offer themselves willingly
in the day of Your power,
in the beauty of holiness *and* in holy array
out of the womb of the morning;

to You [will spring forth] Your young men,
who are as the dew."
Psalm 110:3 (AMP)

It's coming like a lightning storm
Coming like a child's first word
Carried in strength and majesty
Released with love and purity

Your breath across the waters lie
Waiting for no compromise
Within the hearts of heaven's sons
To release the Kingdom Song

Come forth – come forth with the morning dew
Come forth – come forth from heaven's holy womb
We offer ourselves willingly
In the beauty of Your holiness
Come forth! Come forth – Kingdom Song

The day, the hour, is drawing nigh
When ev'ry heart, ev'ry eye

The Son of Man, Jesus Christ
The world can't help but recognize

Don't look back, prepare the way
Throw off the weights, don't delay
The north, the south, east and west
In every field – The Great Harvest is here
        It's here – it's here

Come forth – come forth with the morning dew
Come forth – come forth from heaven's holy womb
We offer ourselves willingly
In the beauty of Your holiness
Come forth! Come forth – Kingdom Song

We're here to buy gold refined
Salve for eyes, garments white

Let Your Kingdom come!

Led With a Purpose

"Then Jesus was led by the Spirit
into the wilderness
to be tempted there by the devil."
Matthew 4:1 (NLT)

There's something so powerful about being stopped in your tracks by the Word of God. It's happened to me countless times over the years, yet I never tire of it.

I remember the first time Matthew 4:1 had that effect. I remember who I was with, where I was sitting, and even the discussion we were having. I remember because I was so shocked by what I'd just read.

"Then Jesus was led by the Spirit into the wilderness to be tempted there by the devil."

What? Jesus was led *by the Spirit* into the wilderness? It was like a curtain had blown back for a second and I glimpsed a side of my God I didn't know existed.

I couldn't believe I'd missed it before, but there it was. Jesus didn't just bump into Satan while walking through the desert. The devil didn't sneak up on Him when His Father wasn't watching. No, this was a divinely inspired season, planned and arranged by the Father.

After that fact sunk in for a moment, a second startling thought came to my mind: The Holy Spirit is *still* leading us into wildernesses to be tempted by the devil.

Although a bit disconcerting at first, a calm settled over me as I realized the value of our times of testing.

We're not just floating around, open prey to the enemy. There are seasons appointed by the Father when we will be tested by the devil for a greater, much greater, purpose. A purpose so important, in fact, our Maker wants to make sure we don't miss it so He leads us there.

Proverbs 17:3 (NLT) tells us, "Fire tests the purity of silver and gold, but the Lord tests the heart."

Our Creator doesn't do anything randomly. He *always* has an objective. He *always* has a plan. And part of our journey will include tests of the heart.

With this backdrop set, the Holy Spirit continued to build in me an understanding of His refining fire of love in the coming years – through the Word, trials, and His faithfulness.

Verses like James 1:3-4 (AMP) set a joyful goal before me:

> "Be assured *and* understand that the trial *and* proving of your faith bring out endurance *and* steadfastness *and* patience.

> But let endurance *and* steadfastness *and* patience have full play *and* do a thorough work, so that you may be [people] perfectly and fully developed [with no defects], lacking in nothing."

Many other scriptures gave strength to endure:

> "For no temptation (no trial regarded as enticing to sin, no matter how it comes or where it leads) has overtaken you *and* laid hold on you that is not common to man

> [that is, no temptation or trial has come to you that is beyond human resistance and that is not adjusted and adapted and belonging to human experience, and such as man can bear].

But God is faithful [to His Word and to His compassionate nature], and He [can be trusted] not to let you be tempted *and* tried *and* assayed beyond your ability *and* strength of resistance *and* power to endure, but with the temptation He will [always] also provide the way out (the means of escape to a landing place), that you may be capable *and* strong *and* powerful to bear up under it patiently." I Corinthians 10:13 (AMP)

"And after you have suffered a little while, the God of all grace [Who imparts all blessings and favor], Who has called you to His [own] eternal glory in Christ *Jesus*, will Himself complete *and* make you what you ought to be, establish *and* ground you securely, and strengthen, and settle you." I Peter 5:10 (AMP)

You aren't tempted by God – God is incapable of being tempted by evil and He Himself tempts no one. (See James 1:13.) Rather, you are tempted when your own evil desires and passions draw you away. Even then your Creator doesn't look at your sin, error, and weakness and throw up His hands in despair.

In fact, He's not even surprised.

He knows we need a Savior and a Redeemer. And so He leads us to opportunities of healing and freedom – seasons where light will shine in our dark corners, painful and embarrassing as it is, yet with the promise of mercy and grace from One who understands, personally, the assaults of temptation.

The One who overcame all things helps us overcome as well. What hope. What amazing wisdom. What love.

"Blessed (happy, to be envied) is the man who is patient under trial *and* stands up under temptation, for when he has stood the test *and* been approved, he will receive [the victor's] crown of life which God has promised to those who love Him." James 1:12 (AMP)

Life is in the Light

"The night is almost gone, and the day is near.
Therefore let us lay aside the deeds of darkness
and put on the armor of light."
Romans 13:12 (NASB)

Ever get a glass splinter in your finger? You can *feel* it – it even alters how you use your hand – but you can't *see* it. In fact, sometimes you have only a general idea of where it is.

Not until you hold your finger under a lamp and let the light glint off of the shard will you really see what is there. Only then can you gently remove it with a pair of tweezers.

The spot may be sore for a while, but the relief is immediate.

How about those little splinters hidden in your soul? You know: the ones that cause you to react abrasively or avoid certain activities or people?

Tiny shards altering what you do or how you live. You can feel them, but can't quite see them. You know they're there, but aren't always sure how or when you picked them up.

Ignoring these hidden irritants lasts but a while and trying to dig them out causes yet more pain. Only one solution will work: Light. In sitting still before our Creator – in prayer, in the Word, in worship, in quietness – His light reveals secrets of the soul.

I've meditated on Psalm 43:3-4 (AMP) dozens of times in the last eight or ten years:

"O send out Your light and Your truth, let them lead me; let them bring me to Your holy hill and to Your dwelling…"

As I cried out, *"Father, shine Your light; Holy Spirit reveal Your truth,"* unexpected deception was exposed, unknown heartaches uncovered, and un-confessed sin revealed within my soul. Some closer to the surface than I realized; some buried so deep I could have never found them on my own.

Gently, perfectly, He removed each one as I held still.

Facing dark corners and hidden secrets isn't easy, but until you do you're destined to live out of the fruit of your darkness.

In contrast, daylight brings you to a point of decision where you can no longer make excuses or justify your choice to continue in error.

Light exposes for the express purpose of freedom and healing.

While we would never think of leaving a glass shard in our finger once we discover it, how often we fight exposing the hurt or sin deep within.

One of Satan's most devastating lies is that God will reject you if you come into the light – if your fear, sin, shame, or pain are exposed.

Nothing could be further from the truth.

- Jesus encouraged His disciples to walk in the light so darkness wouldn't overtake them. (See John 12:35.)
- In John 8:12 (ESV) Jesus proclaimed, *"I am the light of the world. Whoever follows me will not walk in darkness, but will have the light of life."*
- In Romans 13:12 (NASB), Paul exhorted the Roman believers with these words: *"…let us lay aside the deeds of darkness and put on the armor of light."*

Darkness overtakes to do harm; Light offers the gift of life.

Darkness leaves you dry and weary; Light releases refreshing spring rain.

Darkness holds in bondage; Light brings freedom and healing.

Darkness weakens to death; Light protects as a heavenly armor.

If ever there were direct opposites, this would be it. And if ever you're longing for relief, run into God's presence. His light always brings Life. Amazing – yes – but forever true.

> "I have come as Light into the world so that everyone who believes in Me will not remain in darkness."
> John 12:46 (NASB)

> "But you are a chosen race, a royal priesthood, a holy nation, a people for *God's* own possession, so that you may proclaim the excellencies of Him who has called you out of darkness into His marvelous light;"
> I Peter 2:9 (NASB)

> "For once you were full of darkness, but now you have light from the Lord. *So live as people of light! For this light within you produces only what is good and right and true.*" Ephesians 5:8-9 (NLT, emphasis mine)

Lifting My Gaze

"Many are saying of me,
There is no help for him in God.
Selah [pause, and calmly think of that]!

But You, O Lord, are a shield for me,
my glory, and the lifter of my head."
Psalm 3:2-3 (AMP)

There's something about the morning after a storm.

Fog hangs low on the mountains as the sun slowly burns holes through to the valley below. Colors are vibrant and wet as the smell of earth permeates the air.

This morning was one of these. After a pounding thunder and rain storm last night, today awoke with the freshness of new life.

I was up much of last night, pressing in to agree with my Father's heart for friends and family who are in pain and bondage. I also felt the weight of my own weakness and sin in comparison to the One I follow.

Yet with the sunshine coming over the hills, my hope is renewed and strengthened. In Christ, all things are made new.

Everywhere I turn I'm seeing "The best is yet to come" – the very words the Spirit started my year with. I'm grabbing onto them again. I'm letting Him lift my gaze to see the beauty ahead.

What I see with my physical eyes isn't the whole story.

Our God is doing much in each moment – with each agreement to His Word.

No night is ever so long or storm so dark that His Life cannot burn through.

Be encouraged! He's not finished with us yet!

Light Exposure

"And the Light shines on in the darkness,
for the darkness has never overpowered it..."
John 1:5 (AMP)

It may have only been a piece of candy, but it stands forever in my memory as the first thing I stole. And even though I was just four, somehow I knew to hide it from Mom.

When I tried to hide *myself* in the floorboard of the car she became suspicious. Moments later I was marching back into Ben Franklin's to apologize and give back my treasure.

It seems like a funny childhood story but I wonder:

How do we know at such a young age to hide our sin?

Although I grew up in a Christian home, I doubt I had any concept of the word *sin* at this point. Clearly I knew I'd done something wrong, though. I didn't want to get caught – or lose the candy hidden in the dark clutches of my little hand.

What about you? Do you remember those times of blaming a little brother or sister for leaving the wet towel on the bathroom floor when it was most definitely your towel? Or how about running through the house yelling, "He hit me!" when you poked him first? We all have our childhood stories.

But then we grew up and were soon stuffing bigger secrets into darker corners as they no longer fit into our tightly clenched fists.

Instead, we carried lies within the closets of our mind; hid attitudes and opinions behind a smile or a joke; and habits were lived out in the secrecy of our car or behind the building. Practices we didn't want anyone to see.

It's interesting that the first recorded words God spoke at the creation of our universe were *"Let there be light."* He separated darkness from light and created the first day.

Fast forward about 4000 years to John the Baptist and another Light coming to the world:

> "John himself was not the light; he was simply a witness to tell about the light. The one who is the true light, who gives light to everyone, was coming into the world." John 1:8-9 (NLT)

Again light was to shine upon the earth, but this time through the life of Jesus.

This Light would expose darkness in the hearts of men. Jesus didn't come to the world to judge us, but to save us. Yet many reject Him and hate His Light for fear of their sin being exposed.

I've been there. You have too. You don't want to get caught. You don't want to admit what you've done. You want to hide it just a little longer so you don't have to deal with it.

But here's an important piece of the picture:

> Light shines to make *all* things visible. Sin – yes. But also the lie, the snare, the scheme that drew you into the sin. Light exposes your enemy.

When you step forward, into the light of Jesus, you step into truth. Yes, your dark secrets and dirty laundry will be exposed. But so will the lies that got you there and the traps you fell into while stumbling around in the dark. Mindsets that have led you down dead-end roads will also be revealed.

Light isn't meant to shame you, but to free you. As the Savior of the world, Jesus' light brings the healing balm of love, not guilt.

Do you want to see how you've been lied to by the deceiver of this world?

Do you want to be free?

Truth isn't always easy, but it always leads to joy. Light unveils a love that is your destiny and your Friend. This is amazing news!

> "...So live as people of light! For this light within you produces only what is good and right and true."
> Ephesians 5:8-9 (NLT)

Love from a Higher Perspective

"'And you must love the Lord your God with all your heart,
all your soul, all your mind, and all your strength.'

The second is equally important:
'Love your neighbor as yourself.'

No other commandment is greater than these."
Mark 12:30-31 (NLT)

Love. Possibly the most written about, sung about, and desired aspect of our existence.

No matter the culture, background, age, or income, I've never met a man, woman, or child who didn't have a deep, internal longing to be cared for. Even if they initially push others away, behind the walls and beneath the pain and fear lie hidden, but very real, desires to be loved.

We all have ideas or notions about how love should look or feel. Some are based on God's Word; some are influenced by the world around us. Even if we choose to live a life of loving others, how do we define exactly what that looks like in the mass array of circumstances in which we find ourselves?

Even in the Christian community, we often quote well-known scriptures, but how do they play out in our everyday lives?

A few months ago I read the story of Lazarus. (See John 11:1-45.) I've heard or read this story dozens of times over the years, but this time one word jumped right off the page at me: *Therefore.* It looks like a pretty harmless word, but it now added a totally new dimension to the story.

> "Now Jesus loved Martha and her sister and Lazarus. [They were His dear friends, and He held them in loving esteem.]
>
> Therefore [even] when He heard that Lazarus was sick, He still stayed two days longer in the same place where He was." John 11:5-6 (AMP)

By this time in His ministry, Jesus was well-known across the countryside for healing the sick, diseased, blind, deaf, and crippled. It would seem an obvious act of love for Him to go to His close friends when He heard one of them was sick.

And to confuse matters even more, we find further into the story that Jesus *knew* Lazarus' sickness would cause him to die.

Yet, here it's recorded that Jesus stayed away *because* of His love. How do these pieces of the puzzle fit together?

Jesus knew something Martha and Mary didn't yet: Genuine love isn't dictated by emotions.

Yes, we may feel a variety of emotions when we walk in love, but there should be only one Guide in our expression of love: the Holy Spirit.

Jesus knew the greatest love He could express to His dear friends was to do what His Father told Him. Although it might seem hurtful to Mary and Martha in the short term, Jesus loved them enough to trust His Father with the bigger picture.

We can see the deep compassion in Jesus' heart as He tried to encourage the disciples, and later Martha and Mary, and then wept at their lack of understanding.

"This sickness is not to end in death; but [on the contrary] it is to honor God *and* to promote His glory, that the Son of God may be glorified through (by) it." John 11:4 (AMP)

"Jesus said to her, Your brother shall rise again... I am [Myself] the Resurrection and the Life." John 11:23, 25 (AMP)

"Jesus said to her, Did I not tell you *and* promise you that if you would believe *and* rely on Me, you would see the glory of God?" John 11:40 (AMP)

Moments later Jesus called Lazarus forth, from death to life, revealing the Kingdom of Heaven.

What circumstances surround you today? Maybe it seems obvious how you should handle them and love those around you. Maybe you have no idea what to do.

Either way, I want to encourage you to take a minute, or an hour, or as long as it takes, and sit quietly with your Father. Let His Spirit speak and give you direction before moving forward.

He may lead you to do exactly what you were planning or He may unfold a bigger, more intricate plan. He often confirms His plans with His Word and through other believers, and they will always be consistent with His character.

God *is* love and His plans and purposes will always reveal this truth in the end. If we leave Him out of the picture, however, I can almost guarantee love will also be lacking. What an honor to be part of His plan.

"...may you have the power to understand, as all God's people should, how wide, how long, how high, and how deep his love is.

May you experience the love of Christ, though it is too great to understand fully. Then you will be made complete with all the fullness of life and power that comes from God.

Now all glory to God, who is able, through his mighty power at work within us, to accomplish infinitely more than we might ask or think." Ephesians 3:16-20 (NLT)

My Permanent To-do List

"Do not be anxious about anything,
but in everything, by prayer and petition,
with thanksgiving, present your requests to God.

And the peace of God, which surpasses all understanding,
will guard your hearts and your minds in Christ Jesus."
Philippians 4:6-7 (ESV)

I confess: I'm a list-maker. I think I enjoy making them almost as much as I enjoy completing them. They keep me organized and in line. Somehow a neat, orderly column pulls an overwhelming task down into the realm of possibility.

A few months ago I made the most important list of my life.

My initial thought was to hang an old marker board in the shower so I could capture writing ideas that might otherwise escape while getting ready in the morning. That plan went quickly by the way-side when the pens wouldn't write in the shower steam.

I soon discovered the Holy Spirit had something better in mind.

Later that week, I found myself wrestling my way through a decision as I cleaned the bathroom. I longed to hear clear instructions from the Holy Spirit but my mind spun in a dozen directions. I needed to bring myself back to ground zero; to get back to the lowest denominator.

I grabbed a couple of the markers and wrote down what has become my permanent to-do list.

These are not new ideas. They are as old as time. I've believed in them and practiced them thousands of times over the years. But there's something very powerful about setting truth as a signpost before you.

- Pray.

Stop. Worship the Creator who knows you by name, sees each breath you will take, and understands every detail of the world around you. Share your day, your circumstances, your heart with Him as you would your best friend. Wait. Be still. Listen. Worship.

- Obey.

If what you hear lines up with the character of God as revealed in Jesus, if it agrees with the truth of God's Word, move forward as He has directed you. Don't put it off. Don't wait until you begin to wrestle with it again. Listen and obey. Quickly.

- Rest.

Set that decision on a shelf. Lean back and take a deep breath. Rest in the safety of God's love, power, and wisdom.

Know He is always and forever lining things up and putting details in order for a perfect purpose. Know He will continue to show you steps as they need to be made and correct you when you start to go off course – as you keep your heart and life soft before Him.

- Believe.

Expect. Look for results. Laugh. Go forward with other tasks and responsibilities, confident the Holy Spirit is doing more than you know to ask. Thank Him for taking care of and leading you every time the issue comes to mind.

- TRUST.

  "And let the peace (soul harmony which come) from Christ rule (act as umpire continually) in your hearts [deciding and settling with finality all questions that arise in your minds...]" Colossians 3:15 (AMP)

Rarely a morning goes by without pulling my day back to this list. In what could become a panic with all that needs to get done, I look up at the board and take a deep breath.

My Father knows what lies before me.
He knows what is important.
He sees the big picture.
He loves to lead me to the other side.

I love that!

How about you? Do you have a special list? How does the Holy Spirit lead you through decisions?

No Mere Man

"No one has ever seen God.
But his only Son, who is himself God,
is near to the Father's heart;
he has told us about him."
John 1:18 (NLT)

What comes to mind when you hear the name *Jesus*?

Maybe you think of His birth surrounded by shepherds, angels, and the smells of a stable. Maybe His painful death upon a Roman cross. Or a resurrection that shocked even His closest friends.

When you hear the name of Jesus, do you recall one of the well-known stories of His life on earth? When He walked on water or turned water into wine? When He spoke to the crowds or rode upon a donkey to the shouts of "Hosanna"?

Maybe this name reminds you that your sins are eternally forgiven and your life is wholly redeemed. Has He healed you or set you free from an addiction? Has He spoken words into your heart leaving you forever changed?

Is Jesus the One who gives you hope to get up each morning?

So many things can come to our minds. I want to encourage you: This list should never be put on a back shelf or become stagnant, but continue to grow longer each day as we continue to grow in awe and wonder of this One, Jesus.

I grew up in a Christian home and have read the Bible more years of my life than not, but it often takes my breath. It causes all other thoughts to fall from my mind as I am again captured by living, breathing words.

As I read and re-read them, up and down, back and forth, I try to soak in every drop of their residue. I underline and circle and highlight as they take on meaning beyond what I am able to express.

Then I lean back and release a long sigh, once again in love with the Author of such a Book.

I woke in the night last week and went up to my prayer room. I had barely started reading in Colossians when I found myself captivated again. So much was packed into just a few verses. I'd like to share them, maybe to add to your list.

- "[Now] He is the exact likeness of the unseen God [the visible representation of the invisible];" (1:15)

- "He is the Firstborn of all creation." (1:15)

- "For it was in Him that all things were created, in heaven and on earth, things seen and things unseen, whether thrones, dominions, rulers, or authorities;" (1:16)

- "All things were created *and* exist through Him [by His service, intervention] and in *and* for Him." (1:16)

- "He Himself existed before all things…" (1:17)

- "…and in Him all things consist (cohere, are held together)." (1:17)

- "He is also the Head of [His] body, the church; seeing He is the Beginning, the Firstborn from among the dead, so that He alone in everything *and* in every respect might occupy the chief place…" (1:18)

- "For it pleased [the Father] that all the divine fullness (the sum total of the divine perfection, powers, and attributes) should dwell in Him permanently." (1:19)

- "And God purposed that through (by the service, the intervention of) Him [the Son] all things should be completely reconciled back to Himself, whether on earth or in heaven..." (1:20)

- "...through Him, [the Father] made peace by means of the blood of the cross." (1:20)

- "In Him all the treasures of [divine] wisdom (comprehensive insight into the ways and purposes of God) and [all the riches of spiritual] knowledge *and* enlightenment are stored up *and* lie hidden." (2:3)

- "For in Him the whole fullness of the Deity (the Godhead) continues to dwell in bodily form [giving complete expression of the divine nature]." (2:9)

Jesus may have walked the earth in a man's body, but He was no mere man. He carried within Himself the fullness of the Father's love, wisdom, and power that we might know the mysteries of the Kingdom of God.

I encourage you to meditate on these verses. Ask the Holy Spirit to fill you with wisdom and understanding into the deep treasures they hold.

May we be full of the Hope who is our Salvation – the River of Living Water for all who thirst.

Nothing Else

"As the deer pants for the water brooks,
So my soul pants for You, O God."
Psalm 42:1 (NASB)

Gentle deer, tender hart
Looking for a mountain brook
Gentle deer, tender hart
Nothing else can satisfy – can satisfy

Forgiven one, peace you've found
Pressed against your Savior's heart
Much esteemed, delightful one
Nothing else can satisfy – can satisfy

I only tell of what I've seen
I only tell the thing I know
From the Father's breast
Christ, You came to give us hope
And hope fulfilled

   And only You can satisfy
   Only You can satisfy
   Only You – can satisfy

Opportunity for Needed Change

"Pray like this:
Our Father in heaven, hallowed be Your name.

Your kingdom come,
Your will be done,
on earth as it is in heaven."
Matthew 6:9-10 (ESV)

What used to be hidden from all but the wise and discerning should now be painfully obvious to most everyone:

All gray areas are quickly disappearing.

You must know what you believe, what you are willing to fight for, and why. And not making a decision *is* a decision.

Until recent years, I hadn't really thought of myself as a fighter.

Although my generation grew up in relative peace and comfort, I've come to see that at some point limits will be pushed until a stand *must* be taken. This isn't bad, just reality.

Knowing precisely where you stand on an issue is necessary and good. As history has shown, comfort often breeds complacency. Ease produces apathy. And before long, the few – the minority with far-reaching theories and ideologies – push to the top and suddenly unimaginable ideas become tolerable, then probable, then normal.

And then, as struggle is often a great teacher, conflict is often the great divider – separating the pure from the vile – giving opportunity for needed change.

If you know me personally or through my writings, you know I value waiting upon the Lord. Sitting before Him in quiet trust is our strength and roots often grow deepest when adversity drives us to this place.

It's important to remember, however, roots grow in order to produce fruit and true faith results in action.

As we come to know our God deeper and deeper, we begin to share His heart and desires. He fills us with the same passions He carries. Rarely does passion result in stagnation; it motivates to movement.

As members of the Body of Christ we can no longer hide in the background. We can't think everything will be ok without our input or participation.

Our God doesn't sit still. He is active each and every moment bringing about purposeful change. Not a second is wasted or unimportant. He despises not the small things, but builds His Kingdom on these.

We must be of the same mind.

Not everyone's actions will look the same. The scope of our Lord's plan is immense with countless elements. We won't know our part, nor have the grace and courage to fulfill it, unless we sit quietly with Him.

But as He speaks, as He points, we must step forward to do His bidding.

Steal away with your Creator. Then rise up to represent Him and bring His Kingdom on earth.

It is our calling. It is our destiny. It is our responsibility.

Prayer From the Wilderness

"As for me,
I shall behold Your face in righteousness;
I will be satisfied with Your likeness
when I awake."
Psalm 17:15 (NASB)

As I was writing one morning, I pulled out a box of old journals. I grabbed a few random notebooks in search of a particular event, but came across this entry written in the early morning hours a few years back.

It's one of those prayers from deep within – deeper than we understand. It carries a unique mixture of brokenness and strength only the Spirit of God can reveal in us. May it minister to you if you find yourself in a wilderness full of questions and tests.

Our Father always has the perfect reason for leading us there and the perfect plan to bring us through.

* * *

It matters not what was or what shall be. It matters what is this very moment. And this very moment I lean, I trust, I cling to the Word, my Lord, and believe in Your unending and all-encompassing love and forgiveness towards me in my present state.

I do not wish to excuse my behavior. I do not wish to go back and try to redeem it. Only You can do that in Your sovereignty and love. All I know is my heart is broken before

You. I feel like a lost soul, wandering aimlessly, not sure what to think or do with this moment.

Yet, all I can think is how much I need You – how You're the Rock I need and cling to.

So I step under the flow of Your magnificent grace and let it wash over me. I close my eyes and let it run gently over my face and heart and life. I stand under the cleansing flood of Your blood and Your love knowing nothing is more powerful or effective towards Life.

Do You know my love towards You, my Lord?

You must, as You know *all* things, and yet it's so deep beyond me, I feel I don't even know its depths. So truly, You alone know me. You alone – not even I – know what lies within the deepest reaches of my heart and soul.

And I have to trust You are making me what You want me to be.

I declare Your righteousness over me in Christ Jesus. I declare Your redemptive power and strategy. I declare Your promises unending. I declare Your love, intimate and burning.

I declare my devotion to Your pleasure. I declare myself to be in Your grace and favor by Christ Jesus. I love You as I know how, and beyond.

I don't know how to walk each day – only that You do, so I must walk with You. I will not fear but will stay close and trust Your mercies and protection.

Though my heart tries to overwhelm me, I will cling to and rest in Your love towards me, knowing You would not deceive or harm me. You will not refine me in this fire one moment too long or too short, but to the perfection of Your Son.

Today, again and again, I yield to this place and time and purpose that I may be a praise and honor and glory to You and Your Son. Though I know not how or when, I will rise from this place with great joy, proclaiming Your goodness to all, stripped of the old, standing in the new.

I love You.

Real Change

"You have a strong arm;
Your hand is mighty, Your right hand is exalted.

Righteousness and justice are the foundation of Your throne;
Loving-kindness and truth go before You."
Psalm 89:14 (NASB)

Some years ago I began praying for my nation. Maybe you have prayed these words as well:

"Father, bring truth.
Bring justice.
Reveal all hidden things.
Let Your Kingdom come."

Every time I said those words, however, I had this nagging feeling I wasn't only praying it for my nation *but over myself.*

If God is going to reveal truth, if He's going to bring justice and righteousness to the earth, none of us is exempt from His refining fires. While we may have someone else in mind when we think of who needs to change and get right with God, He knows the deep cracks and crevices of every heart.

Even mine.

Even yours.

Change doesn't start out there on some distant platform or committee. It doesn't even start with the person standing next to you.

Change – *real change* – starts at the core of your being; it starts when you encounter the One who created you and you can no longer stand any essence of yourself that varies from His holiness.

All those issues we ignore in ourselves but underscore in others – pride, envy, selfishness, greed, impatience, anger, dishonesty – His fire will reveal and consume in each of us without exception.

All those secrets we think are forgotten or hidden deep enough to maintain our current life, His light will expose so they no longer have room to grow and undermine His Life living through us.

That's what a prayer for change – a prayer for justice and truth – will do. You'll get what you ask for, starting with you. He will come so close as to feel His breath as He speaks words of love and comfort, but also the fire of His holiness as He purifies your thoughts and intentions.

I can say from experience, the refining fire isn't easy. It's real. It's brutally honest. It's painful.

But the results are *very* exciting.

When you ask for truth and justice no matter the cost, when you let the Holy Spirit speak exactly what He wants to you and you *still* press further into His chest, something powerful happens.

You begin to *see yourself* for who you truly are – both the beauty and the sin – and you *experience God* for who He truly is.

Your Creator. Your King. Your Savior. Your Healer. Your Beloved. Your Friend.

In ways deeper than you could ever imagine He becomes your grace. Your courage. Your hope. Your freedom. Your joy. Your peace.

Your everything.

And then you start to see others the way He sees them, in the reality of their pain, torment, fear, and loneliness. You see weary, hurting, confused people, but through the lens of His love and hope.

When you and I stop pointing at all the things *out there* that need to change and realize the real change needs to happen in our own heart, our own actions, words, and life – that's when God is able to do great things.

Ephesians 3:20 says He is able to carry out His purposes and do far above all you could ever dream or hope for – when His power is at work within you.

Now that's exciting!

Don't let impossible looking circumstances discourage you. Let the Holy Spirit do the impossible in you. Then He can do the impossible through you.

He is the change we all need.

"To get nations back on their feet, we must first get down on our knees." Billy Graham

Self-surgery

"Be still in the presence of the Lord,
and wait patiently for Him to act..."
Psalm 37:7 (NLT)

Sometimes the most productive thing you can do is be still.

Don't move or speak or even think if it takes you down a rabbit trail of answers and questions and answers and questions. Those spirals may lead somewhere eventually, but the cost far out-weighs the benefit.

No, sometimes your best input is to rest.

To trust.

To listen.

To soak in the words and works and faithfulness of Another.

I've learned this many times through experience, but gained a better understanding in a recent dream.

I saw myself on an operating table. It seemed a tumor needed to be removed and, as crazy as it sounds, I was performing surgery on myself. As I lay on my back with shoulders up and neck cricked, I opened up my abdomen.

As I stood on the outside, watching myself, I thought, *"That's just crazy! I/she can't see what she's doing. She's going to cut out too much or leave something that needs to be removed."*

The whole thing was so obviously foolish.

Then above it all, You spoke:

"Yes. So why do you try to do what only I can do? I know all and see all the healing that is needed. What needs to be removed and sewn up.

Lean back, rest, and let Me change you. Let Me heal you. I do it perfectly. Just rest."

"...For I am God, and there is no other; I am God, and there is no one like Me." Isaiah 46:9 (NASB)

Simple Words

"He sent His word and healed them,
And delivered *them* from their destructions."
Psalm 107:20 (NASB)

Simple words, falling down – gentle drops of rain
Pierce my heart, burn my soul – speaking hope again

Your simple words – oh, they're falling down
Like gentle drops of rain
They pierce my heart and they burn my soul
You're speaking hope again

>When You speak, Lord, all time stands still
>My every storm must cease
>Your simple words, oh, my heart's convinced,
>They're heaven's greatest gift

I'm waiting here, in the dark
I know Your light will shine
When words of truth pierce the night
Bringing hope again

>When You speak, Lord, all time stands still
>My every storm must cease
>Your simple words, oh, my heart's convinced,
>They're heaven's greatest gift

Spot On

"Thus says the Lord,
In an acceptable *and* favorable time
I have heard *and* answered you…"
Isaiah 49:8 (AMP)

God's timing is so perfect, down to the millisecond. He's never late, never early. His timing is neither random nor accidental – He's spot on.

I find we often push the envelope in an effort to get Him to move faster or catch up to us and our plans. But then we learn: Faster is not always better.

I experienced a simple but telling object lesson recently. My husband, Matt, and I have raised chickens for a number of years and the time had come to butcher the older hens and order new chicks. With each attempt to call the hatchery I was met with the beeping busy signal.

It's so rare to get a busy signal anymore; I'd almost forgotten what they sound like. But each time I hung up, went back to the catalog, and re-checked my order. And every time I found a new option or piece of information about availability I'd missed before.

Each and every time I made important adjustments to my order.

By the afternoon, I began to think my call might never make it through, but tried one more time. This time a very friendly lady answered the phone and something clicked in my spirit:

If she would have answered any of my other six calls, I would not have been fully prepared. Without all of the necessary information I would have gotten what I asked for, but not what I wanted or needed.

How often we cry out to God, "I'm ready! Let's go!" Yet we truly don't know what our next breath will hold, let alone the next mile. Crucial pieces of the picture, pieces we may never see, are still being put into place. People, places, plans, provision: The Holy Spirit is the Master Builder.

I had to remind myself of this truth again this week.

I've been working on another book off and on for the last couple of years. I told myself it would be done this summer. Summer is winding down, though, and I'm more than a few thousand words from the finish line.

My days have overflowed with good, important tasks and the Holy Spirit has unveiled several surprise events at the last minute. I haven't been sitting around wasting my days, but the last few months have definitely not looked like I thought they would. It's easy to get anxious about what I think I should be doing.

Do you ever feel the tug of the calendar? Do you keep counting back the days to see how long it's been? Or how long you have left until a deadline?

It only takes a glance in the direction of panic and soon you're entertaining it in your living room.

But while you worry and fuss and try to figure out how to make it all happen the Holy Spirit is wisely and meticulously putting details in order, helping you leave unnecessary luggage behind, teaching you to trust Him in greater measure.

Each moment is a precious gift; every hour more important to the Holy Spirit than we know.

- May He seal in our hearts each object lesson of patience.

- May we treasure each step as a gift rather than striving and reaching over it to the next.
- May we find the joy and rest He's leading us to by knowing He is perfectly wise, absolutely good, and completely powerful.

Strive to Rest

"Let us therefore be zealous
and exert ourselves *and* strive diligently
to enter that rest [of God,
to know and experience it for ourselves],

that no one may fall *or* perish
by the same kind of unbelief *and* disobedience
[into which those in the wilderness fell]."
Hebrews 4:11 (AMP)

Resting is an interesting concept.

You could probably ask a hundred people what it looks like to them and get a hundred unique answers.

At different points in my life I might have pictured reading a good book while the kids were asleep, a week at the beach, or waking up refreshed.

Others would say, "A day off of work," or "The feeling after a project is finished." All of these would fit into the definition of rest, in both the English dictionary and in the Bible.

Our human bodies need consistent blocks of time to recuperate after a day or season of activity. When Jesus walked the earth, He regularly took time away from serving the crowds and urged His disciples to do the same. This *anapauō*[9] type of rest is a ceasing from labor in order to recover and regain our strength.

Another type of rest, however, far surpasses a temporal, physical recuperation.

Katapausis[10] (pronounced kä-tä'-pau-sēs) does not depend on our level of activity, remaining constant even when the body is exhausted. This rest doesn't hinge on governmental peace or if we live in abundance or lack. *Katapausis* is a resting place during the greatest storm; a peace unshakable.

I recognized glimpses of it as I read the words of Katie Davis in her book *Kisses from Katie* this week.

In the midst of thousands of starving, hurting people in Uganda, this young lady strives to look past the vastness of the task, beyond the impossibilities surrounding her, and into the truth of who Jesus is. She walks out one day at a time, obeying His leading while relying on His goodness, strength, wisdom, and power.

And at the end of the day she looks back with joy beyond understanding at all of the mighty things He has done.

As the world seems to be going faster and faster and the trials and tribulations increase with each passing year, having a higher level of rest available to us is of irreplaceable value. Yet, it doesn't come without a cost. The author of Hebrews urges us to strive diligently to enter this rest.

What does this mean? How do we *strive to rest*?

- First, one of our highest priorities should be to have a soft heart before God.

  "Therefore, as the Holy Spirit says: Today, if you will hear His voice, do not harden your hearts, as [happened] in the rebellion [of Israel]…" Hebrews 3:7-8 (AMP)

A soft heart is an open heart.

A soft heart is vulnerable and honest, allowing God to show the truth about Himself, our soul, and our circumstances. It is often painful, but only in this place can we avoid devastating lies and snares of our enemy and instead walk in the joy and freedom God desires for us.

If we push certain sins and issues back in the corner in an effort to hide or not deal with them, our hearts will become more and more hardened and deceived by sin. We begin to think *we* know how best to live out our lives. This pride and rebellion will separate us from the One who is our only hope of peace.

- Second, we must obey what the Father tells us through His Word and by His Spirit.

  "So God's rest is there for people to enter, but those who first heard this good news failed to enter because they disobeyed God." Hebrews 4:6 (NLT)

Obedience is the litmus test of humility.

A step of obedience reveals our heart hasn't completely hardened against God and opens us up to see the loving sovereignty of our Maker.

In obedience we come to recognize and accept a God who knows all things and moves in perfect wisdom, power, and love.

I John 3:24 encourages us to obey God's commandments as a means to remain in fellowship with Him. I love the picture the Amplified Bible paints: "They let Christ be a home to them and they are the home of Christ." In this close communion, *katapausis* rest can be found.

- Third, we must come to a place of absolute trust in God alone.

  "For only we who believe can enter his rest…"
  Hebrews 4:3 (NLT)

God doesn't ask us to have blind faith. He constantly shows Himself to be perfectly wise and powerful. In this way we are meant to mature in our trust of Him.

Although the Israelites left slavery in Egypt with many great signs and wonders, they failed to enter into the rest God desired for them because they didn't come to a place of trust.

When difficult circumstances arose, they quickly fell back on their own understanding instead of placing their faith in the faithfulness of their Savior.

They believed in their own weakness more than they believed in the power and goodness of God.

We are faced with the same dilemma today. To enter into the fortress and hiding place of peace, we must choose to look beyond physical circumstances to the truth of who God is. We must choose to rely upon His goodness, wisdom, and power when all of the facts around us yell out that failure is imminent. We must choose to put our faith in God over the cries of our emotions or weaknesses.

This choosing may start out as a gritting of the teeth and a holding on with all we have, but as our God reveals His faithfulness over and over again, we learn to lean back into Him and truly rest. Even smile at the process.

Now, before we get too overwhelmed at what we must strive to do, read further in Hebrews 4. Our Father doesn't leave us to work these details out on our own.

- First, He gives us His Word – alive and full of power, sharper than any two-edged sword – to expose, analyze, and judge the very thoughts and purposes of our heart.

We don't have to wonder what's right or wrong. When we read the Word of God in humility and hunger, the Word itself will penetrate into our hearts and reveal within us what must remain and what must be changed.

- Second, God gave us His Son, Jesus, Who has shared in all of our weaknesses and assaults to temptation, and so understands what we are walking through.

Because He walked in perfect relationship with the Father and without sin, He is able to give us mercy in our failures and grace to help with every need. He beckons us to come fearlessly, confidently, and boldly to His throne.

"Striving to rest" seems like an oxymoron. But as we lay aside pride and live before our God with a soft heart, as we exchange our sin and rebellion for His plans and purposes, as we believe He loves us perfectly and can be trusted explicitly, we find a place of rest no one can take away.

In this rest Paul wrote letters full of hope and thanksgiving even while sitting in prison.

To this rest David returned in Psalm 55:23 after wrestling with his fears.

And into this rest our Father calls us today. Amazing.

Such a Voice

"I went to sleep,
but my heart stayed awake.

[I dreamed that I heard] the voice of my beloved…"
Song of Solomon 5:2 (AMP)

Words of love, words of life
Like warm oil pouring over me
Breaking, healing, capturing my soul
    I will follow, I will follow
    Looking, longing for that Voice of love

I will wait, I will dance
I will sing knowing that You will respond
I long to hear it, won't You sing along
    Nothing else will do
    Won't You sing – won't You sing, Jesus
    Won't You sing again with me

Such a Voice I've never heard before
Such a Voice – it shakes me to the core
You sustain me, You entice me
Sing again to me sweet melodies

Words of love, words of life
Like warm oil pouring over me
Breaking, healing, capturing my soul
    I will follow, I will follow
    Looking, longing for that Voice of love

Such Love

"In the beginning was the Word,
and the Word was with God,
and the Word was God.

He was in the beginning with God.

All things came into being through Him,
and apart from Him nothing came into being
that has come into being."
John 1:1-3 (NASB)

As I read John 1 this morning a wondrous, terrible thought cut me again to the core:

The perfect One, the One who created all things, *knew* when He created man that we'd turn against Him.

He knew when He said "*It is very good*" it wouldn't remain so. He knew the beauty and perfection of nature would degenerate as sin entered the world. He knew His prized possession – mankind – would reject their Maker and hurt themselves and each other to unimaginable depths.

Jesus knew as He spoke creation into existence He would lay down His authority and take on the limits of a human body. He understood the cost of walking among those He created to make a path back to His Father.

He *knew*, yet He spoke.

He *knew*, yet He moved forward in His plan to have sons and daughters with whom He would share His life, wisdom, love, and power.

How did You feel as You were speaking creation into existence, Jesus? How were You able to do it?

Father, was there pain in Your heart at that moment knowing Your Son would walk the earth, rejected and scorned?

When You looked down through time and saw death, painful death, did you hesitate?

Or did You stand firm, knowing Jesus would rise and defeat death with death?

Oh Lord, may my life be a fragrant offering of thanksgiving back to You. May I be a vessel through which You can pour Yourself out and reveal Your heart of intimate power.

May this child, this lump of clay so perfectly formed, bring You love and honor through the grace of Your Son. May I be a piece of Your redemptive plan to defeat evil and expose Your wisdom and truth.

May love consume and guide me. May joy extend its hand through me. May Your Kingdom dwell richly in me that the greatness of Your love, patience, long-suffering, kindness, grace, and peace be recognized and known.

To You be all glory and honor, power and dominion forever. To You alone, for You alone are worthy.

From the highest in the land to the babe now taking his first breath, may You be seen in perfect truth and love.

That Smile

"In the light of the kings' countenance is life,
And his favor is as a cloud bringing the spring rain."
Proverbs 16:15 (AMP)

When You walk into a room,
the night turns into sunshine.

And when You speak my name,
no matter how far down I've fallen –
 Your breath of Life begins to flow and
 fill my lungs again with hope.

That smile, that laugh, even through my tears I see
Your joy, Your confidence, and I know all is well.
Then I can't help but rise above this rainy day.
That smile I love – always puts me on my feet again.

 Though the night is almost over
 Sometimes I think I can't go on.
 But a look, a touch, a word and
 I know I'll make it to the end.

That smile, that laugh, even through my tears I see
Your joy, Your confidence, and I know all is well.
Then I can't help but rise above this rainy day.
That smile I love – always puts me on my feet again.

 I am on my feet again.

That You May Know

"I do not cease to give thanks for you,
remembering you in my prayers,

that the God of our Lord Jesus Christ, the Father of glory,
may give you the Spirit of wisdom and of revelation
in the knowledge of him,
having the eyes of your hearts enlightened,

that you may know
what is the *hope* to which he has called you,
what are the *riches of his glorious inheritance* in the saints,
and what is the *immeasurable greatness of his power*
toward us who believe..."
Ephesians 1:16-19 (ESV, emphasis mine)

Ephesians is an amazing book.

I can easily spend months at a time pondering its timeless words, rolling them over and over in my heart. I often find myself praying Paul's prayers for the early Church over myself and others, gently holding each syllable like a drop of honey on my tongue.

This past week I was praying them over myself.

As old habits and emotions tried to pull on me, I pressed in to hear the Spirit. He said, "*Read Ephesians.*" Such perfect guidance.

In praying for eyes to see the hope to which I'm called and the greatness of His power in me, I was again overwhelmed at the One I serve. In ways too deep to express

He has renewed my thoughts simply by showing me more of Himself.

This Christian walk, I've found, is a unique and precise tension between having eyes to behold the wisdom and glory of God and a heart that hungers for yet more.

If we could easily see and understand all of who our God is, we would just as easily dismiss Him. If His vast mountain of wisdom, love, and power could be scaled in a single day with the ease of a Sunday stroll, we would never comprehend the depths of His endless riches.

In the tedious, in the gut-wrenching, in the struggle to continue we learn the value of hunger.

To the comfortable and satisfied, even the slightest discomfort is anguish. But to the hungry, a trek through the wilderness is forever worth the table set on the other side.

Spiritual hunger is a precious gift from a Creator who knows our weaknesses. To be hungry is to be motivated; to be hungry is to need something outside of ourselves.

Hunger drives us beyond the empty pleasures and pain of earth into knowing the eternal realms of heaven – and that while still on earth.

With profound understanding Jesus spoke to the crowds: "*Blessed are those who hunger and thirst for righteousness...*" (Matthew 5:6, NASB) He knew the pull of complacency and the value of desire. He knew without hunger we would just as soon sit in our mess.

But Jesus also knew the importance of desires being fulfilled: "*...for they shall be satisfied.*"

In all of our longing, we must be able to recognize God to be satisfied.

If the Holy Spirit were to only tempt you on without profound moments of rest and dining with Him, if you never experienced the unspeakable joy of seeing His personal involvement in your journey, if the truths of the Bible didn't come alive and active in your own life, you would certainly become heartsick.

Without His power strengthening you – body, soul, and spirit – you could soon lose faith and fall deeper into despair than at the first.

Yes, this road is narrow and difficult that leads to Life, but it is *abundant* with the things of heaven. There is satisfaction with each step when your eyes are fixed on the Perfect One. With one glimpse of His smile, one word from His lips, one touch of His hand, your heart is strengthened and your desire to continue to the end deepens.

What an amazing revelation: Jehovah God is both the longing *and* the reward.

In gazing upon His beauty you will find both hunger *and* satisfaction.

- Where does today find you?
- Are you weary or overwhelmed?
- Have you settled into a deep, dry rut?
- Do you still believe, but need a fresh word?

As Paul prayed from a prison cell nearly 2000 years ago, I pray for you now:

- May Light from heaven shine on your heart even this moment and give you fresh wisdom and revelation of your Father.
- May hope rise up within – hope in the perfect union between you and your God.
- May the rich inheritance of His presence and power overwhelm you – exciting and enabling you to be and do more than you have ever considered before.
- May the same faith that filled and motivated Jesus to follow each and every word of His Father also fill you, bringing the Kingdom of God into your circumstances.

The Amazing Gift
of God's Love and Life

> "For God loved the world so much
> that he gave his one and only Son,
> so that everyone who believes in him
> will not perish but have eternal life."
> John 3:16 (NLT)

John 3:16: Probably the most well-known verse in the Bible.

Many of us memorized it as children, listening again and again as it was quoted in sermons or Sunday school classes. Usually, the following picture was painted:

> Believe Jesus is God's Son, ask Him to forgive you of your sins, and you'll live forever in heaven after you die.

This is true.

But it's kind of like saying, "The Bible is a good book." Yes, that's true too, but it just barely touches the surface of the truth. The fact that John 3:16 is such a familiar verse shouldn't keep us from gaining all the riches these few words contain.

- First, I want to look at the preface of this verse – "For God loved the world so much…"

This must be the foundation of our walk with Jesus. Any deviation will surely set us on shaky ground.

God didn't send His Son to the earth because He was angry with us, and Jesus didn't come to point out our faults or make us feel guilt and shame. John 3:17 clearly states Jesus didn't come to judge, reject, or condemn the world, but that the world would find salvation and be made safe through Him.

Our Creator isn't sitting up in heaven, holding a big stick, looking for ways to punish us. Rather, His every thought and action is directed at revealing His great love and mercy, wisdom and power.

I love Ephesians 2:4-5. If ever I question God's heart toward me, these verses secure me again in the truth. The Amplified Bible says it this way:

> "But God – so rich is He in His mercy! Because of *and* in order to satisfy the great *and* wonderful *and* intense love with which He loved us,
>
> Even when we were dead (slain) by [our own] shortcomings *and* trespasses, He made us alive together in fellowship *and* in union with Christ..."

Did you catch that? *To satisfy His great and intense love* He made us alive when we were dead.

I remember the first time I read those words. I stopped short and re-read it to make sure.

I'd grown up hearing God loves me, but for my salvation to somehow satisfy His intense passion for me – what an overwhelming thought. May all I do be built upon this truth.

- This takes us to the second nugget in John 3:16 – "...that He gave His one and only Son..."

There's one distinct difference between Jehovah God and all other gods: The God of Abraham, Isaac, and Jacob gave of Himself to make a way for us to be with Him.

No other god, no other religion, has ever given so deeply in order to redeem its followers from death. On the contrary, all other gods and religions require your life, your time, your money, your devotion, and your sacrifice.

Jesus is the only God who came to earth and gave His *life* so that we might gain *His Life.*

- Third, "...so that everyone..."

Jesus offers redemption to all. He loves without prejudice or boundary.

In fact, Jesus seeks out those we would consider to be the least desirable or deserving. He chooses the weak and weary, but doesn't ignore the rich and powerful. He calls all who are in need, without discrimination.

In John 7:37, Jesus stood before the crowds and made this amazing invitation: "*If any man is thirsty, let him come to Me and drink!*" Any man. No exceptions. Jesus came to give life to all.

- God's only requirement is the fourth piece of truth: "...who believes in Him..."

Belief is an interesting thing. So many people say, "Yes, I believe in God," but in reality they believe little more than a God exists somewhere, out there. They've never submitted their heart and lives to Him.

Biblical belief goes much deeper than a head nod. It is a leaning of the entire being onto Another. It is a bending of the will to the authority and plans and working of that One.

Belief in Jesus is a daily walking out your life with Him, listening, obeying, changing (inside and out), and allowing Him to love you to your core.

It is giving up death in exchange for Life, Himself.

- This is what John had in mind when he finished with "(they)…shall not perish but have eternal life."

Jesus gives us the definition of eternal life in John 17:3 (AMP):

> "And this is eternal life: [it means] to know (to perceive, recognize, become acquainted with, and understand) You, the only true *and* real God, and [likewise] to know Him, Jesus [as the] Christ (the Anointed One, the Messiah), Whom You have sent."

Eternal life isn't just something we receive after we die; it's a gift we begin to open the moment we believe, trust, and rely on Jesus.

Eternal life is a personal, growing, intimate, never-ending relationship with our Creator. It manifests itself as peace in the midst of a storm, grace to obey, forgiveness and freedom from sin, love everlasting, joy even in pain, and more. Much more.

When Jesus invited all who were thirsty to come and drink, He concluded with these words: "*He who believes in Me [who cleaves to and trusts in and relies on Me] as the Scripture has said, from his innermost being shall flow [continuously] springs and rivers of living water.*" John 7:38 (AMP)

Eternal life is just that – the life of God pouring through us forevermore.

The depths of God's riches in Christ Jesus are inexhaustible. There are dozens of verses to expound on each of the truths put forth in John 3:16. May this short description serve to whet your appetite to dig yet further into the amazing gift of God's love and life.

The Joy of a Father's Discipline

"My child, don't make light of the Lord's discipline,
and don't give up when he corrects you.
For the Lord disciplines those he loves,
and he punishes each one he accepts as his child."
Hebrews 12:5-6 (NLT)

I have so many great memories of my dad.

- Sitting side by side on the piano bench as he played and I plunked;
- working together in the pig barns;
- snacking on peanut butter and saltine crackers;
- swinging under the apple tree;
- enjoying the mellow sounds of his western guitar and vocals.

I also have precious memories of time spent with my heavenly Father.

- Sharing the excitement of the first wildflowers in spring;
- waking up to the moonlight on my face;
- hearing His internal whispers as I pray for others;
- sitting in the spray of a waterfall as I imagine His voice like the sound of many waters.

The lists could go on and on.

My most treasured memory, however, is not of the laughter or celebrations or sense of wonder. My most valuable memory is when both my dad and my Father spoke truth that shook my world to its foundation.

I'd allowed my heart and life to become entangled in relationships that were silently killing me and my family. I knew it deep inside, but didn't have the courage to face the truth.

At just the right moment, in a gentle but firm word, my dad spoke what I couldn't and opened a door to freedom.

At the same moment it felt as if my heavenly Father grabbed me by the collar and pulled me back from the edge of a cliff. In a flash He opened my eyes to see details I'd missed for so long. I had chosen to follow my fear instead of believing in the love and faithfulness of my God.

In tender but strong words the Holy Spirit disciplined me.

It was a fearful, gut-wrenching day. It's not easy to stand before a Holy Father and realize your sin. As scripture after scripture filled my mind, they exposed my heart and separated lies from truth. The sword of the Word cut to the deepest purposes of my heart.

It was also painful to face the family I love when I had failed so miserably. But I will forever treasure that moment. Both my Father and my dad loved me enough to risk offending me in order to save me from much greater pain.

Much of society scoffs at the idea of discipline, believing the only way to show love is by acceptance and praise. I agree love always believes the best and works to build others up.

There are times, however, when love must speak truth in order to correct, teach, and discipline.

I'm like anyone; I usually prefer applause over correction. But I've tasted the joy of a Father's perfect training. Its sweetness is eternal.

Hebrews 12:10-11 tells us God's discipline may seem painful at the time, but is always for our good.

His discipline allows us the miracle of sharing in His holiness.

Rarely a day goes by that my heart doesn't swell with thanksgiving and wonder for the day I was offered freedom and healing. This invitation often comes with correction, but oh the joy of knowing you're a child who is loved.

The Joy of His Presence

"The heavens declare the glory of God;
the skies proclaim the work of his hands.

Day after day they pour forth speech;
night after night they display knowledge."
Psalm 19:1-2 (NIV)

As I write this, birds sing in a great chorus outside my office window. Sunshine slides down the hills and through the Aspen leaves, and the smell of dew is still in the air.

So many reminders of the One I love.

About fifteen years ago, I began walking each day. What started as a young mom's desire for a few minutes alone turned into a treasured routine.

I hike most every morning, first thing, when the air is cool and the bugs are asleep. I cherish time alone with the Holy Spirit – to listen, learn, see, and understand what would otherwise get lost in the busyness of the day.

I laugh with my Creator while watching birds chase each other around and through the trees. I marvel at the vast array of grasses and wildflowers. I catch a hint of His power when thunder roars on the horizon.

And as rain bounces off my face, eventually giving way to a brilliant bow across the valley, I'm reminded of His unending faithfulness through the storm.

Some mornings, as dozens of cars rush by me on the way to work or play or appointments, I wonder if the people riding inside see the long shadows on the hillsides or the eagles flying overhead.

Do they notice the river is clearing and the balsamroot are in bloom? Do they recognize the Spirit pulling them closer to the One who created all these? Do they see His wisdom and truth in His handiwork?

I wonder:

> Has modern society lost a measure of its spiritual awareness because we take so little time to walk?

In not allowing ourselves time to slow down, to be close to the earth around us, have we become impervious to a God who chooses to reveal Himself through His creation?

I know many who are reading these words live in cities, surrounded by concrete and steel. I lived in Manhattan, NY, for a year and a half during my college years. It was a very different world from my homes in Montana and Wyoming.

Still, every chance I could get I walked the city streets, always returning to my apartment with my mind and heart full of new-found treasures.

One of my favorite memories is when I came out of a late-night prayer meeting in the Empire State Building. I stepped outside to an empty street and the low, smooth sounds of a saxophone. Sitting all by himself, an older black gentleman filled the air with the most beautiful melodies for an audience of countless unseen angels.

As I explored Central Park or Greenwich Village, I never tired of the variety of faces and eyes and smiles; of tasting new foods and finding hidden park benches with elderly men playing chess. I heard languages from around the globe and saw cultures in mini-segments.

So many celebrations of the fingerprints of God.

Although the mountains and vast open spaces were thousands of miles away, I quickly learned the Holy Spirit could reveal enough about the Father in a patch of grass and a butterfly to fill my heart and mind for days!

Today, in the midst of life, I encourage you to take time out to walk. Park a few blocks away from your appointment. Explore a new part of town. Check out the bike path or nature trail. Let the Spirit refresh and strengthen you with the wisdom and beauty that surrounds you.

Let the earth and sky reveal to you the invisible qualities of your Maker.

> "No wonder my heart is glad, and I rejoice... You will show me the way of life, granting me the joy of your presence and the pleasures of living with you forever." Psalm 16:9, 11 (NLT)

The Longest Day

"Then Jesus shouted out again, and he released His spirit.

At that moment the curtain in the sanctuary
of the Temple was torn in two, from top to bottom.
The earth shook, rocks split apart, and tombs opened.
The bodies of many godly men and women
who had died were raised from the dead."
Matthew 27:50-52 (NLT)

I woke this morning pondering "the day in between".

The crowds had all gone now. Joseph of Arimathea had taken Jesus' body the night before, wrapping it in clean linen before placing Him in a new tomb. The stone had been rolled across the entrance as Mary Magdalene and the other Mary watched.

Now it was the Sabbath and they must rest. They must wait.

The pain and agony of the trial and crucifixion must have been beyond all we can imagine. Watching as the One who had spoken life and wisdom from heaven hung silent before the chanting crowds. Dying.

And then His last breath, His last cry, as darkness fell upon the land, *"Eli, Eli, lema sabachthani?"* – "My God, My God, why have You abandoned Me?"

Usually this is where we take a break in the story, picking it back up with the two Mary's going to the tomb early Sunday morning.

But what about the day in between? The longest day?

Imagine the silence. The confusion and unanswered questions. Minutes ticked by like dripping water. One at a time. Endless hours of wanting to say something, but not knowing what.

Nothing to do now but wait. Nothing to do but try to keep hands and minds busy with the tasks at hand. One foot in front of the other. One minute after another.

Ever have a day like that? A day after hopes have died. A day when confusion replaced dreams. Where silence felt thicker than the earth's crust and each breath weighs like a stone upon your chest?

> *"We must have misunderstood. We must not have heard correctly. I guess God didn't really mean what He said."*

I know I've had those days. I doubt many reading this haven't.

And yet, those longest, darkest days have served to do more for my faith than any of the bright, sunny ones. The darkest hours have produced the greatest fruit of strength and endurance.

If we have eyes to see and a willing heart, we come to understand: While we're in that thick, crushing silence our God is still moving, still working, still God.

Jesus was no less God in the tomb than when He walked the earth, raising the dead and healing the sick. Neither the circumstance nor the setting diminished who He is. Just the opposite. In the tomb, in the depths of the earth – during the depths of the disciples' despair – Jesus was doing His greatest work.

He was conquering the very thing everyone thought had just conquered Him.

I love Acts 2:24 (AMP): "[But] God raised Him up, liberating Him from the pangs of death, seeing that it was not possible for Him to continue to be controlled *or* retained by it."

Death *could not* hold Jesus.

The Son of God carried the very Life of God. Death *had* to release its hold and bow under Christ's authority.

What about you? What about your dark hours of confusion and death, be it physical, spiritual, mental, or emotional? Where is God then?

- He's working beyond all you can think or imagine.
- He's putting pieces in perfect order for Life to soon spring forth in greater measure than before.
- Life to fill and liberate you *and* all who drink from the cup you hold out to them.

Don't slide back into the corner of your longest day. Bow your heart and soul before Him and let Him fill you with resurrection Life. Let Him minister His hope and peace, for tomorrow will bear the fruit of a God who still works miracles in the dark tombs of our soul.

The Power and Purpose
Of Heaven's Fragrance

"Your oils have a pleasing fragrance,
Your name is like purified oil...

Draw me after you and let us run together!"
Song of Solomon 1:3-4 (NASB)

Little alters one's mood like a pleasing fragrance.

- bread, hot out of the oven
- wet, rich soil
- sun dried towels
- just-bathed babies
- ripe grapefruit
- soft, worn leather
- freshly cut wood
- finely chopped herbs

These cause the soul to pause and remember it's alive.

I love such moments, but more still catching a whiff of heaven.

You know: little reminders of a realm more real than the ground under your feet. Perfectly timed confirmations that you are a new creation, born of the spirit, seated in heavenly places in Christ Jesus. These treasured experiences are meant to reveal more fully the One who is all in all; to unfold Truth; to display the unending wisdom, power, and goodness of Jehovah; and to lead you closer to His gaze.

Sometimes heavenly aromas blow across your path in physical, tangible ways.

We're half-way through summer with signs of fall already showing. But as I walked between thundershowers this morning the Spirit whispered, "*It smells like spring.*"

I took in a deep breath and smiled as He continued.

> "*I can bring springtime to any season. I made the seasons for man, for the earth, but I'm outside of time. I can bring forth Life in any season.*"

As I walked, I recalled priceless moments when God stepped into my winter seasons and planted hope. How He caused dry, harsh circumstances to burst forth with fresh, green growth. And I paused to ponder how He might bring new beginnings in this season.

How many times I've enjoyed the smell of rain, but today He used it to remind me:

> None of life's seasons can stop His Life's intervention.

Several years ago, during an especially difficult time, I began to notice the strong scent of sagebrush surrounding me each morning as I hiked. One day the Holy Spirit whispered, "*That's the fragrance of grace.*"

I would savor the bittersweet smell for hours, often rubbing the leaves between my fingers or breaking off small branches to take home. Inhaling the distinct odor brought comfort and strength as it assured me of a Father who leads us to victory.

In measures I'm still unfolding years later, I've learned:

> God's grace encompasses, turning bitter pain into sweet fellowship.

I wonder if these truths also went through Jesus' mind as Mary poured pure nard on His feet and wiped them with her hair. As perfume filled the room, the fragrance of worship overshadowed His impending pain and prophesied Life that overcomes death. What a precious gift from a loving Father.

Sometimes, no natural cause can explain a specific scent.

- Like a breeze through a window, I've often caught the gentle aroma of kindness or joy or peace when someone walked by.
- While in worship and prayer, I've sensed a residue of smoke and ashes, although no fire was near.
- Sometimes, as I sit quietly in God's presence, a soft perfume fills my spirit.

Although I understand only in part, all of these experiences point me to Jesus. All of them draw me into deeper communion with my Father.

All of them reveal the One who became a sweet fragrance and calls us to the same. (See Ephesians 5:1-2.)

The Power of Light

"This is the message we have heard from him
and proclaim to you,

that God is light,
and in him is no darkness at all."
I John 1:5 (ESV)

Imagine a place with *no darkness*. None. Not even a shadow. Only constant, pure, powerful light.

- Revealing truth.
- Giving security.
- Bringing warmth.
- Producing growth.

This is the nature of our God, our Creator: "*...in Him is no darkness at all.*"

Now imagine a place with *no light*.

- Black, murky, cold.
- Lifeless and without distinction.
- The words *heaviness* and *hopelessness* come to mind.

There's nothing warm or inviting about this scenario.

Light and darkness: Polar opposites; two incompatible conditions.

Light is foundational to life, as revealed in our Creator's first recorded words: "*Let there be light.*" And in a moment a dark, empty wasteland transformed into a target of potential. (See Genesis 1:3.)

This initial light wasn't from the stars or sun or moon, as many of us assumed before reading more thoughtfully. No, these cosmic spheres were created three days later.

This first light appeared when God released Light from within Himself. The "no darkness at all" lit up this darkened planet.

Genesis 1:4 goes on to say God saw that the light was good and suitable, and He approved it. Then He separated the light from the darkness.

Most of us have read or heard this story of creation, but what does it have to do with us now? We *have* light and dark, night and day, so what more do we need to know?

> The God who first released Light into darkness... is still doing so.

Have you ever walked into a darkened building – one you'd only seen from the outside?

At first you carefully make your way around from the little bit of light that shone in when you entered. But that soon dissipates and although nothing but ebony lies ahead, you feel compelled to explore. To just see what's around the corner.

"*I can always find my way out,*" you think.

But the further you venture into the center of the structure, the more you bump and stumble and bruise shins. You may even fall down a set of stairs or knock something over, causing others to get hurt.

Soon you find yourself beat up, lost, and desperately wishing for a light switch.

Although I've only experienced a portion of this scenario in a dark building, I've experienced it to greater degrees than I'd like to admit in the circumstances of life.

- I've walked into situations I knew were dark and unfamiliar.
- I've bumped and bumbled my way through, trying not to break something or hurt myself and others.
- I've been torn between going deeper in and trying to find my way out.

Somehow, I thought the darkness would hide my mistakes and cover up my fear and confusion, but they only grew and multiplied. I imagined this unlit path would eventually lead to a desirable place, but it only thickened like quicksand around my feet.

Only when the Light of truth, the Light of the Holy One, entered into my prison did I realize how much I wanted and needed to be free. I found myself breathing in the Light as if it were air.

Light was the only answer. Light was the only solution.

Without it I wandered aimlessly and without hope. Deceived by my own choices, I could never see my situation accurately or find peace and freedom.

Maybe this sounds familiar. Maybe you're lost in the dark – lost and hurt and confused. This is where the words "*Let there be light*" are hope for you today.

Light *still* radiates forth from your Creator, pushing back darkness and exposing barriers, traps, and hurtles. Light *still* breaks in, revealing injuries and showing the way out.

After walking in the dark for a while, Light can seem so harsh, so blunt. But it is absolutely necessary. And it is good. Light brings hope, and hope leads to freedom and life.

For Light comes not to condemn or judge, but to save.

> "Again Jesus spoke to them, saying, 'I am the light of the world. Whoever follows me will not walk in darkness, but will have the light of life.'" John 8:12 (ESV)

The Rest of the Story

"I know the Lord is always with me.
I will not be shaken, for he is right beside me.

No wonder my heart is glad, and I rejoice.
My body rests in safety."
Psalm 16:8-9 (NLT)

Sometimes the bigger story happens behind the scenes.

One of my favorite memories from growing up is gathering around the radio for the best five minutes of the day: *The Rest of the Story*. Paul Harvey's radio show was loved by an estimated 24 million people every week, at its peak, and I was counted among them.

I loved hearing a story brought to life by the hidden details, details often showing the fingerprints of our Creator.

With that in my mind, I just had to laugh after a radio interview on the Nothing Wavering Show last week. I felt like I'd just walked out of one of Mr. Harvey's stories. You'd think, being a live show, it would've been obvious to listeners what was happening. But once again, my Father revealed Himself in a most precious and powerful way.

Going back in the story a bit, we've had an exceptional amount of static on our land-line the last couple of years. I've had the repairman out enough times that we're now on a first name basis, but to no avail. We still had noise. So as I prepared to do the interview, I was also trying to think of a phone I could use.

My husband, Matt, suggested I ask at our church, since they have more than one line. Our pastor was more than happy to let me borrow his office, so I was in business: A nice, quiet place to do the show.

I arrived in plenty of time to set up my computer and get my notes out. I noticed a prayer group was meeting in the room next door, so I closed the office door so I wouldn't disturb them.

At exactly 9am we went live and the prayer group let out. As the introductory song was playing, they gathered outside the pastor's office to visit as they put chairs and tables back in the racks, totally unaware of what I was doing.

I started to panic as the noise level grew, but the Holy Spirit whispered, *"Don't worry. Just focus."* Turning my body away from the door, I adjusted my attention and let Rita Springer's song lead me into my Father's presence.

Before I knew it Shane Davis had introduced me and I was sharing my testimony.

Then, without warning, another louder sound took over in the hallway: The carpet cleaners had pulled up right outside the office and turned on all of their equipment. Again, my thoughts started to get rattled, but a soft, strong word from the Spirit pulled me back, *"Don't worry. Just focus."*

I sat back in the chair and rested in His word. As I answered questions and shared my heart, I found myself lost in my Father's goodness. In what seemed like a moment we were already to the half-way mark and Shane played another song.

In a text I told him they were cleaning carpets and I hoped it wasn't too loud. His reply: "Can't hear a thing."

I smiled because, honestly, by that time I didn't hear it either.

I'd gotten so lost in the closeness of my Father's presence filling the office it was often hard to speak. In believing and trusting in those few words, *"Don't worry. Just focus,"* I'd somehow stepped into a deep place of His love and I soaked up every drop I could.

When the last words were spoken and the final song was playing, I leaned my head back in amazement: While Shane and I had talked about resting in God's presence, my Teacher, the Holy Spirit, had given me another opportunity to experience what that means in day-to-day life.

As I walked to my car, the carpet cleaners rolled up their hoses. I laughed out loud! How mighty is my God!

When God says, *"Don't worry,"* He knows exactly what He's talking about.

When He says, *"Just focus,"* He will become a resting place, even in a noisy hallway.

Nothing is impossible for our God or for those who look to Him.

The Son's Footstool

"But our High Priest offered himself to God
as a single sacrifice for sins, good for all time.

Then he sat down in the place of honor at God's right hand.

There he waits until his enemies are humbled
and made a footstool under his feet."
Hebrews 10:12-13 (NLT)

As I read the verses above, two details jump out at me.

- First, Jesus is sitting beside the Father in a place of rest.

Looking at the world around us, we may be tempted to become fearful or anxious. As we see more and more of the signs Jesus detailed in Matthew 24, even those who don't believe in Him are taking note, wondering what the future holds.

Although Jesus warns the Church to be sober and alert, holding to truth and resisting temptation, it's important to note *He* is altogether peaceful.

Psalm 37:13 (AMP) goes so far as to say,

"The Lord laughs at [the wicked], for He sees that their own day [of defeat] is coming."

Jesus is not anxious.

He is confident in His past victory at the cross and sure of His future victory through His Word, His Bride, and the heavenly host.

Jesus knows the power of the Father's love and the persistence of the Holy Spirit. He is secure in His Father's perfect plans working out His Kingdom purposes in our individual lives. He is certain of the final outcome of His Church.

He sits in peace.

- Second, Jesus is waiting for His enemies to be made a stool beneath His feet.

A footstool is used to step up to something higher – to reach the next level.

As I pondered this, I believe the Spirit said:

> "*Upon the plans of Christ's enemy shall the Body of Christ step up to become the Bride in fullness and satisfaction.*"

As the Body – with Jesus as our head – we're part of standing on the stool made up of His enemies. All the enemy tries to stack against us will actually be what we step up on to gain the greater faith and maturity spoken of in Ephesians 4.

When we walk through the obstacles of our enemy by the truth, grace, and wisdom of our Lord, they become stepping stones to manifest the glory of Christ upon the earth.

Lord Jesus – by Your grace, through Your righteousness, in Your peace – may Your Kingdom come in fullness in Your Bride.

The Treasure Within

"Whatever is good and perfect comes down to us from God,
our Father, who created all the lights in the heavens.
He never changes or casts a shifting shadow.

He chose to give birth to us by giving us his true word.
And we, out of all creation, became his prized possession."
James 1:17-18 (NLT)

Remember the old saying: "The grass is always greener on the other side of the fence"?

It makes me think of my neighbor's horses, standing in a vast field of hay but straining their necks to reach under the fence and nibble a little grass on the other side.

We all have that tendency, don't we? From childhood all the way through our adult lives, we think those things just out of reach are going to *really* satisfy.

- If I could just take a vacation;
- if I buy that new _____;
- if I get this new job;
- if I can find the perfect someone... I'd finally be happy.

But the truth is, when we get over the excitement of our new experience or purchase or accomplishment, we soon find ourselves reaching under another fence.

Meanwhile, we forget that as Believers we carry within a Treasure greater than all the earth contains.

I love studying the teachings of Jesus. He never offered temporary solutions or momentary gratification. He spoke life-changing words with eternal consequences. He called us out of death and into life. No gray areas. No missing pieces.

When Jesus offered water to the woman at the well, He told her,

> "Those who drink the water I give will never be thirsty again. It becomes a fresh, bubbling spring within them, giving them eternal life." John 4:14 (NLT)

God isn't surprised at your longing.

He created you to be a vessel of His presence. He designed you to carry a perpetual stream of Life-giving Water. When you became His child, He placed His Word and His Spirit within you. The One who holds the universe lives *fully* inside of you.

The Word within you has the power to save, protect, guide, and comfort. The Holy Spirit enables you to do the impossible, hope for the unthinkable, and rest in the midst of any storm.

Now it's your responsibility to turn your gaze and longing away from the distractions of this world and drink of His Life.

Today, pull back from those things that sparkle and try to grab your attention. Receive His forgiveness for straining to fill your longings from the empty wells of this world. Then lean back into the words of the One who made you: *"Come, follow Me."* Truly, you will find all you are longing for.

> "As the winds of time unfold
> Treasures buried in the sand
> Let Your Spirit blow within my soul
> Reveal in me

All of Your majesty
Unfold the treasure within me

Joy explodes within my soul
No earthly words have ever told me
The full expanse of Your great love
Mighty love
Mighty love"[11]

The Yoke of Grace

"Come to Me,
all who are weary and heavy-laden,
and I will give you rest.

Take My yoke upon you and learn from Me,
for I am gentle and humble in heart,
and you will find rest for your souls.

For My yoke is easy and My burden is light."
Matthew 11:28-30 (NASB)

What comes to mind when you hear the word *yoke*?

If not an egg sunny-side up, I'd bet it's a team of oxen trudging their way across a field. Steady beasts of burden plowing up the dry, hard ground.

Being cinched into a yoke isn't an inviting picture. It normally implies a heavy load and hard work – possibly being in slavery or bondage to another. For Jesus to use the picture of a yoke in the same invitation to *"Come and rest"* may seem a bit odd.

It's easy to encourage ourselves or others with the *rest* of God and then skip over the next couple of verses about the *yoke*. But Jesus never spoke out of turn. He chose His words very carefully, listening always to the Father.

The Israelites listening to Jesus speak were painfully aware of the burden they carried. Their lives revolved around a strict set of laws and sacrifices. Everything from eating to work had to adhere to a specific standard in order to be in right standing with God.

Even as sacrifices were made to cover sin, they walked away with the weight of knowing there would have to be another. The standard of the Law was simply unattainable.

In stark contrast, Jesus extends to us an invitation of complete forgiveness, freedom, and rest at the price of His own life, death, and resurrection. Jesus fulfilled the Law's every demand and became the perfect and final sacrifice for all sin, for all time.

In breaking the yoke of slavery to the Law, Jesus now offers you a yoke of grace.

This yoke of grace is truly the most beautiful gift Jesus could give. It is "that which affords joy, pleasure, delight, sweetness, charm, loveliness" (*Strong's Concordance,* G5485).

Maybe you haven't really thought about this yoke before. Or you don't think you're very interested in it. I'd like to share a few things I've realized.

- First, this yoke of grace is a yoke of intimate, personal relationship.

  "See how very much our Father loves us, for He calls us His children, and that is what we are!" I John 3:1 (NLT)

- Second, it's a yoke of relentless love.

  "For God loved the world so much that he gave his one and only Son..." John 3:16 (NLT)

- It is also a yoke of divine unity.

  "The glory which You have given Me I have given to them, that they may be one, just as We are one;

I in them and You in Me, that they may be perfected in unity, so that the world may know that You sent Me, and loved them, even as You have loved Me." John 17:22-23 (NASB)

- Jesus' yoke is a yoke of sovereign wisdom.

  "God's purpose in all this was to use the church to display his wisdom in its rich variety to all the unseen rulers and authorities in the heavenly places." Ephesians 3:10 (NLT)

- It is a yoke of the perfect joy.

  "But now I am coming to you, and these things I speak in the world, that they may have my joy fulfilled in themselves." John 17:13 (ESV)

- It's also a yoke of unwavering peace.

  "I (Jesus) am leaving you with a gift – peace of mind and heart. And the peace I give is a gift the world cannot give. So don't be troubled or afraid." John 14:27 (NLT)

- Finally, Jesus' yoke is one of eternal hope.

  "May the God of hope fill you with all joy and peace as you trust in Him, so that you may overflow with hope by the power of the Holy Spirit." Romans 15:13 (NIV)

This list is certainly incomplete. Still, I hope it serves as a reminder: When you step into the yoke of Christ, you step into life abundant.

No longer must you rely on your own strength or abilities; your own goodness and well-intentions. You have inherited the life of Christ – living in you. Living through you.

> "And now I entrust you to God and the message of his grace that is able to build you up and give you an inheritance with all those he has set apart for himself." Acts 20:32 (NLT)

This Day

"This is the day that the Lord has made;
let us rejoice and be glad in it."
Psalm 118:24 (ESV)

While pondering the New Year, one thought keeps coming: *One day at a time.*

I know this isn't original, but with each day it seems to increase in importance.

- Live *this* day.
- Not yesterday, again.
- Not tomorrow, yet.
- Live *today* – fully, thankfully, without worry or regret.

Live *today* – leaning into the voice of God; laying down what He asks of you; taking up what He requires – knowing these will lead to a life fully His and a destiny fully lived.

Live *today* – one minute at a time, soaking in the sunshine and sounds, the tastes and smells. Breathing in the wonder of what the Holy Spirit is doing *this* moment and how it will build from here into eternity.

Live *today* – thankful for yesterday, excited about tomorrow, but fully engaged in the now. In the chores and the sky and the questions and the people and the pebbles under your feet.

Treasures they are, each and every moment.

Treasures to uncover, examine, and build upon. Treasures we too often leave lying on a dusty path as we hurry and clamber towards the next day or month or year.

The foreword for *The Imitation of Christ* says it this way:

> "How often do we say, and hear others say: 'Oh, if only I could have a little peace!' Perhaps our greatest hindrance to this peace we all desire so much is the constant urge to lift the veil and see what tomorrow will bring. We are surrounded by this attitude; our weather forecasts are all occupied with what is coming next. *So we let today's moments slip by us almost unheeded.*"[12]

If you're feeling overwhelmed right now, lost in a sea of noise... please pause.

Take a slow, deep breath and point your thoughts toward Jesus. Let Him separate the precious from the unnecessary. Let His Word strengthen your heart and fill your mind with peace and truth.

Then, slowly, intentionally, hold His hand and take but one step. It's the only one He's asking of you right now. Take it, savor it, and in that moment be strengthened for the next.

As we walk through this year, may you and I be intentional about living it. Living it fully in the light of the One who made it.

May we embrace each opportunity for laughter, each invitation for adventure, and each tear of healing. May we take each step of forgiveness and engage each lesson of growth. May we savor each of these gifts to the fullest. And in this may we come to know the One who so completely knows us.

"As for God, His way is perfect!

The word of the Lord is tested *and* tried; He is a shield to all those who take refuge *and* put their trust in Him. For who is God except the Lord? Or who is the Rock save our God, the God who girds me with strength and makes my way perfect?

He makes my feet like hinds' feet [able to stand firmly or make progress on the dangerous heights of testing and trouble]; He sets me securely upon my high places." Psalm 18:30-33 (AMP)

Here's to 365 days of fullness in Christ. Amazing things await you!

Those Who Cause
the Earth to Groan

"For I consider that the sufferings of this present time
are not worth comparing with the glory
that is to be revealed to us.

For the creation waits with eager longing
for the revealing of the sons of God."
Romans 8:18-19 (ESV)

We stand on the precipice of a great unveiling.

Since before time began a great dispute – a great battle –
has raged in realms unseen. Not a true struggle in the sense
of two equal opponents; the One has always been superior in
every way.

Only the ability to deceive gives the inferior a foothold
with the sons of man. Although the One displays
overwhelming sovereignty time and again, the weak minds
and souls of mankind continue to be swayed by the schemes
of the lesser.

The earth groans as it watches the rise and fall of many
men and nations. It waits for a specific man – a specific
nation.

It anticipates their unveiling, their release onto the earth.
For where they walk no darkness can stay. When they speak,
no deception can persuade otherwise.

The Life they carry overcomes death on every front.

- These walk through the waters, but are not overcome. They know their God walks with them.
- They stand in the fire, but the flames do not kindle upon them for they have been purified in His love.
- They are mocked and scorned, but think it worthy to suffer for the One to whom they have entrusted their every breath.
- They are not afraid, although confronted on every side, for they know the faithfulness and fortitude of their Salvation.

The earth anticipates these, for they carry within the One, Jesus, to whom the earth owes its very existence.

Although there have always been "the faithful" in the midst of trials and Light in even the deepest darkness, this unveiling will be like no other.

Why?

It's like asking, when filling a glass with water, *"What makes one drop any different from the others?"*

At some moment the glass will be full. At some moment it will overflow.

And at a moment unlike any other in history, darkness will reach a point of overflow. But, according to God's great plan, Light will also pour forth in unprecedented display.

Jesus spoke continually of the Kingdom of God being hidden for a season only to be revealed in fullness – as seeds planted in the ground, as leaven in flour. All God has been planting and perfecting from the first day will mature to fullness at the ideal time.

In hiddenness the Lord pours Himself without measure into those whose hearts are pure before Him; those who wait in quiet expectation. At some moment, these hearts will overflow upon the earth – not because they are great or strong, but humble, full of Truth and Peace.

This release will not be a trickle, but a deluge. It will flood the earth as in Noah's day, but with Life and Liberty.

Hold on to this truth.

Hold on to the whispers of the Spirit in the night.

As you walk in humility and love, His Light will break forth in your darkness. You will be revealed as His child and will join with all of His sons to show forth the One who has always been superior.

Time to Go Deeper

"So commit yourselves wholeheartedly
to these words of mine.
Tie them to your hands and wear them
on your forehead as reminders.

Teach them to your children.
Talk about them when you are at home
and when you are on the road,
when you are going to bed
and when you are getting up....

so that as long as the sky remains above the earth,
you and your children may flourish
in the land the Lord swore to give your ancestors."
Deuteronomy 11:18-19, 21 (NLT)

(Journal entry: 12 January 2013; 4:38 a.m.)

"I've been up for a couple of hours. Praying. Seeking.
Meditating.

I'm realizing again, but to a new degree, how
important meditation is. Meditating on Your Word,
on You, on the things You show me. To hold and
study and savor. To let them soak in and saturate my
mind and soul.

Not to "glance in a mirror and then walk away and
forget," but to study and remember and be
transformed.

This is a year of deeper transformation. Deeper meditation. Taking full possession of the treasures You have given me."

Meditation isn't a real common word in churches today. Sometimes I think it even scares a lot of Christians; many think of it only in terms of eastern religions or the New Age movement, not realizing Jesus lived a life of deep meditation.

"Jesus said to them, 'My food is to do the will of him who sent me and to accomplish his work...

Truly, truly, I say to you, the Son can do nothing of his own accord, but only what he sees the Father doing. For whatever the Father does, that the Son does likewise.'" John 4:34; 5:19 (ESV)

Simply put, meditation is the concentration of thoughts on one thing; to think about something *carefully, calmly, seriously,* and *for some time.*

Jesus' whole life focused on His Father. On His words, His plans, His will. Jesus spent much of His time surrounded by people, but He often slipped away to be alone with His Father, later teaching or displaying what He received during these private encounters. Although He lived a very public life, Jesus drew strength, direction, and pleasure from these intimate moments.

If thoughts and words were physical objects, meditation would be the act of holding, examining, taking apart, tasting, smelling, listening to, and savoring in order to study and become one. And in becoming one, to live out what you're focused on.

I've experienced weeks and months of concentrated lingering in God's presence, pressing into His Word, and listening intently for His every whisper. I couldn't run into my prayer room fast enough, nor stay long enough. Everything I learned and treasured from those moments leaked out on the rest of my day. Wherever I went, these lessons expanded and grew deeper roots into my soul.

Suddenly, scriptures I'd heard for years came to life. Knowledge turned into experience. Experience turned into passionate conviction.

As I walked by the river each morning I'd pick up stones to represent what the Spirit was teaching me that day. A small metal box now holds these priceless reminders like treasures found at sea.

Again, the Holy Spirit is drawing me to deeper waters. Again I am reminded: We don't bear the image of Christ by accident. We don't produce fruit, heal the sick, and set captives free by glancing in the Word and walking away.

We don't release the glory of God by focusing on the world.

This year, let's go deeper in God. Let's linger. Let's soak Him in. Let's drink from the bottom of the ocean instead of sipping from the surface.

> "Deep calls to deep at the roar of your waterfalls; all your breakers and your waves have gone over me. By day the Lord commands his steadfast love, and at night his song is with me, a prayer to the God of my life." Psalm 42:7-8 (ESV)

To Know the Mysteries

"I tell you the truth,
unless a kernel of wheat
is planted in the soil and dies,
it remains alone.

But its death will produce many new kernels –
a plentiful harvest of new lives."
John 12:24 (NLT)

I've found myself pondering a lot this week.

Just barely a week before He hung bloody and beaten on the cross, Jesus told His disciples: Unless a kernel of wheat dies, it remains alone.

But they didn't understand. They didn't see.

Mary, overcome by love and destiny, came to Jesus during dinner a few nights later – not privately, but before raised highbrows and scornful thoughts. Taking a pint of precious perfume she knelt before Him, broke the jar, and poured it over His feet. She then wiped them with her hair.

"...And the whole house was filled with the fragrance of the perfume." John 12:3 (AMP)

But they didn't understand. They didn't see.

Knowing it was time to leave this world and return to His Father's side, knowing the disciples would each fall away in one degree or another, Jesus took off His garments, fastened a servant's towel around His waist, and washed the dust from their feet. In shock, Peter protested.

"No! You will never wash my feet!" John 13:8 (NLT)

Peter didn't understand. He didn't see.

Over and over Jesus spoke of His impending death and resurrection. Over and over He spoke of a Kingdom bigger than earth could hold, a Life that conquers death, a Joy that perseveres through pain. Yet His followers were unable to comprehend the unfolding journey.

A journey that would forever change their hearts, lives, and futures.

This has me pondering:

- How many times does the Holy Spirit speak to me, to you, and we don't hear?
- How many clues do we miss?
- How often must He repeat Himself until I understand – or do I completely miss what He's saying until I find myself in a daze, wondering where He is and what just happened?

The day Jesus' crucified body lay in a tomb – the day of confusion, questions, and fear among His disciples – was also the eve of His victory over death.

Same day, same event: two very different perspectives.

Father, may we have ears to hear what You're saying. May we have eyes to see what You're doing.

When You show us the mysteries of Your plan, may we learn to recognize Your ways.

May we see a seed going into the ground and discern a plentiful harvest in our future.

May we be found waiting at the tomb, expecting Your triumphant resurrection.

Two Sides of Betrayal

"Let this same attitude
and purpose *and* [humble] mind
be in you which was in Christ Jesus:
[Let Him be your example in humility]…"
Philippians 2:5 (AMP)

An empty religion will betray itself in relationships.

Just eight words, yet startling in their accuracy.

We can *say* all kinds of things. We can make believe like we believe, but when we rub elbows with the people in our lives, what we *really* believe often becomes more apparent than we'd like to admit.

Still other times, purity of heart is revealed when we walk through dark nights together.

It was Passover. Jesus knew the time had come to return to His Father. He also knew Judas would betray Him in a few short hours for 30 pieces of silver and a misguided motive. It is here we read these remarkable words:

"And as He had loved those who were His own in the world, He loved them to the last and to the highest degree." John 13:1 (AMP)

Jesus taught the greatest commandment: Love. But He did more than teach.

Knowing Peter would deny Him three times and His closest friends would scatter; *knowing* Satan had already put the thought of betrayal in the heart of Judas Iscariot; *knowing*, Jesus continued to love.

In an act as purposeful as any He'd ever taken, Jesus took off His garments, fastened a servant's towel around His waist, knelt down, and began to wash the disciples' dusty, dry feet.

The same feet He created.

The same feet He walked beside.

The same feet He would bleed for and later shod in peace.

I can only imagine the gentleness with which He cupped the water; the slow, purposeful movement of the towel as He wiped off the moisture. Love in every stroke. Painful love.

Love that would be betrayed, yet reveal its purity in such a test.

Have you been betrayed? Have you felt the sting of rejection and loss?

> "Let this same attitude *and* purpose *and* [humble] mind be in you which was in Christ Jesus...
>
> ... (who) stripped Himself [of all privileges and rightful dignity] so as to assume the guise of a servant..."

- Believe your Father's plan is perfect in love, wisdom, and power.
- Obey each whisper, even when it looks foolish.
- Pursue harmony and peace.
- Press in to gain the greater victory.
- Trust. He is doing more than you see.

You will face the test – more than once.

Will your relationships uncover an empty religion? A belief in word only? A core still painfully yours?

Or will your relationships prove to be opportunities to love in spite of pain? To display the beauty, wisdom, and grace of the One who lives within?

"Now to him who is able to do immeasurably more than all we ask or imagine, according to his power that is at work within us, to him be glory in the church and in Christ Jesus throughout all generations, for ever and ever! Amen." Ephesians 3:20-21 (NIV)

Unfailing Expectation

"O my God, my life is cast down upon me
[and I find the burden more than I can bear];

therefore will I [earnestly] remember You..."
Psalm 42:6 (AMP, emphasis mine)

How often we find ourselves looking at our burdens, our problems, instead of looking at the Answer.

No problem exceeds the wisdom of our Creator-God. No issue is too great; no frustration too complicated. Look up and you will see the confident, smiling face of One who is ready to take the burden, take the cares, take your hand, and lead you through.

"[What, what would have become of me] had I not believed that I would see the Lord's goodness in the land of the living!

Wait *and* hope for *and* expect the Lord; be brave *and* of good courage and let your heart be stout *and* enduring.

Yes, wait for *and* hope for *and* expect the Lord!"
Psalm 27:13-14 (AMP)

We Want to See!

"Lord," they said, "we want to see!"
Matthew 20:33 (NLT)

How often we dispense value through a murky lens.

- "*That* job is way more important than *this* one."
- "I accomplished *so* much more yesterday than today."
- "If I can just get *this* project done the day won't be lost."

The roller-coaster ride of feeling a success or failure is exhausting.

I'm a writer.

At least that's part of who I am.

I'm also a wife, mom, friend, cook, gardener, bed-maker, teacher, musician, pillow fluffer, encourager, and lover of books, art, and smoothies. I walk as much as I can and often sit for no reason except to listen to the wind or watch the sky.

I love early mornings – watering flowers and talking to the chickens, cat, and dogs – and making others smile.

Hanging laundry on the clothesline makes me smile. Watching God being God *really* makes me smile.

Mostly, I'm a worshiper.

Sometimes I place too much value on one task while minimizing others. As a writer, if I don't produce a certain amount of words on a regular basis I start to think I'm failing overall. *Failing? Really?*

Yep.

One afternoon as I pulled weeds and mowed grass, shook out rugs and wiped off counters, I wondered at the insignificance of my tasks. I lamented not being able to work on my next book or at least a blog. You know: something important.

Have you ever heard the Holy Spirit laugh? It's stunning.

Not laughter of ridicule or even amusement, but tender joy. Laughter knowing a treasure lies in the path ahead. Laughter at the thought of Truth being uncovered.

Our Creator wants us to see clearly.

To understand mysteries.

To discern value from His perspective.

And so He began to speak.

- *Writing* inspired words is far-reaching, but so is *living* them.
- *Teaching* on My goodness is important, but so is *enjoying* Me.
- Serving *the masses* is noble, but also *the one* with whom you live.

Each breath, each moment is one to cherish. Each step, each person, each action a treasure.

We like to categorize people and things and activities in order of importance. And granted, some things are frivolous and need to be acknowledged as such. But every step given to the leading of the Holy Spirit carries eternal value.

Jesus lived 33 years on earth. Not every day, every chore, or every word made the headlines. Yet each built upon another and carried immeasurable value in the whole.

Your choice to wash the dishes honors all who live in your home. Your decision to be steadfast and honest in your work reveals God's Kingdom. Your joy at the simple things delights the One who pours out His rain upon the earth.

Each task carries worth. Every day holds value in unique, precious ways. I'm choosing to get off the roller-coaster of thinking one day is a failure and the next a success.

Want to join me?

Father, may we hold dear what You hold dear. May we see the small deeds in light of Your wisdom. May we rest in the eternal picture, knowing You are doing more than we can imagine by Your power at work within us.

May we laugh more, cry more, close our eyes and enjoy more knowing each of these is part of the whole. May we give ourselves fully to each moment, seeing them as You do.

What We Already Know

"...let us hold true to what we have already attained
and walk *and* order our lives by that."
Philippians 3:16 (AMP)

Yesterday I woke with a heaviness that just wouldn't budge.

My body tried to resurrect pain from past years and my mind overflowed with an endless list of chores. I was tempted to pull the covers up and fall back asleep but knew if I didn't take a stand right away this wave would drag me under.

With the sun slipping over the hills and a cool breeze whispering through the window, I wrote out declaration after declaration in my journal. Verses that would be familiar to young Sunday school children, yet never diminish in power.

With each stroke of the pen, my spirit revived and my focus was renewed. As I stood on tested, solid ground I felt my legs gain strength and I understood what the Holy Spirit had been hinting at for weeks:

> Sometimes, to overcome a hurdle before us, we don't need to search for new truth or understanding of God so much as we need to live out what we already know.

I love receiving new revelation from God. *Love it.* I love searching out the mysteries of His Kingdom. I long to know this One I serve more intimately with each breath – and I believe He longs for it as well. But lately the Spirit has been reminding me of truths that have long sustained me. Truths I hold like treasured friends.

Unfortunately, over time we can become complacent about our relationships with treasured friends. Sometimes we take them for granted, losing sight of their value. In the same way, we often become complacent about biblical truths we feel are obvious or immature.

For the last few weeks, the Holy Spirit has been pressing me into Philippians 3:16.

"Hold fast to what you've already attained Amy.
Don't forget the things I've taught you"

Every time I'd turn around I'd see a note scribbled on a scrap of paper on my desk: *Live according to what you already know.*

Imagine it.

Imagine if we all walked according to what we've already been taught. The Church currently has more books, music, and teaching available to it than at any other time in history. The Holy Spirit is moving and speaking constantly. We are saturated with truth.

But do we look like what we've learned?

If the Body of Christ lived in the fullness of what we know to this point, we would be an unstoppable force against darkness and a credit to the God who created us.

It's not that you stop pursuing God and deeper understanding. Not at all. In the two verses before (Philippians 3:14-15), Paul encouraged the believers at Philippi to press on to the goal to which God was calling them – to press on to the heavenly prize in Christ Jesus. Paul's own life displayed a determined purpose to progressively know Christ more intimately each day.

But in your pursuit of new discoveries, may you truly walk in the love and grace of Christ. May you obey His commands with humility and joy. May you believe and display the majesty of His wisdom. May you hold fast to and walk in the truth you have attained thus far.

The world around us needs it and Christ deserves it.

When God Speaks

"And the Lord came and stood
and called as at the other times,
Samuel! Samuel!

Then Samuel answered,
Speak, Lord, for Your servant is listening."
I Samuel 3:10 (AMP)

There's nothing quite like hearing the whisper of God.

It reminds us we're not alone. One greater than us is near – nearer than we could imagine.

I seem to find myself in an almost constant conversation with the Spirit on most days – asking what I should do or what He thinks. Sometimes we simply share the excitement of moment by moment discoveries and celebrations.

I often pause and smile at the wonder of it.

If someone were to ask a few years ago, I might have said it's in my prayer room or on morning walks where I most clearly hear His words to me. Maybe even at a benchmark where I often pray or in the quiet hours of the night when I can't fall back to sleep.

It wasn't until my husband, Matt, left town for a week that I realized one of the sweetest treasures God had given to me: the kitchen.

Being alone for a week, I didn't do a whole lot of cooking. A bit of tuna salad, some fruit, and a smoothy here and there. It seemed like such a nice break from the routine of wondering what I was going to make for dinner. I enjoyed having extra time to spend at other projects, but time passed,

Matt returned home, and we were back in the routine. Monday evening: making dinner again.

As I moved from cupboard to cupboard pulling out ingredients and utensils, a sweet sound interrupted my silent thoughts.

A calm, gentle Voice spoke clean, simple truth and made my breath catch in the back of my throat.

I paused, smiled, and continued with the process of dinner. But as I worked, we visited. About the day. About dinner. About a piece of wisdom He'd just lodged in my spirit. About things that would draw me yet deeper into His written Word and later become food and drink when I was feeling overwhelmed or weary.

Before I knew it, dinner was made and on the table.

No one would have known how holy that hour had been. How precious. And suddenly a light burst into my heart: Some of the most profound, most cherished times with my Lord have been while chopping, stirring, and washing my way through a meal.

Amazing. This God who made us, the One who longs for our devotion and friendship, loves to spend time where we are. In the middle of our day, the middle of our routine, the middle of life.

This God makes a precious altar of fellowship wherever we give Him opportunity.

When I Forget
What God Says About Me

Jesus:
"Just as the Father has loved Me,
I have also loved you; abide in My love."
John 15:9 (NASB)

Do you believe what God says about you?

That you're the apple of His eye? That you make Him dance and sing? That He's *always* had you on His mind?

You capture His heart with one glance, you know.

He thinks you're beautiful. He loves the sound of your voice. He knows you're smart. His eyes light up as He prepares your destiny. He's building you into a beautiful tower of strength and love, and He delights in the process.

He's gone ahead, planning each of your steps for good, and invites you to join Him. He prepares joy and peace in the midst of every circumstance because He wants you to truly know Him.

Do you believe it? Do you *embrace* it?

I believe it, but sometimes the way I think shows I don't believe it as much as I want to. As much as I could.

When I get tired. When I grow weary. When I agree with discouragement. When my surroundings pull my gaze away from Him, I forget what He says about me.

- I forget His love knows no bounds, no limitations, no conditions.

- I forget His peace is always within me; I must choose to let it *fill* me.
- I forget His greatest joy is my leaning into Him.
- I allow doubt to suffocate my anticipation of good.

But this doesn't hinder You, Abba.

You don't get distracted or discouraged or lose perspective. You still love me fully, faithfully, without wavering. You still hold my destiny in Your heart, drawing me to You that I may see it too.

You don't give up on me.

You continue to speak and laugh and believe in Your own goodness. You continue to train me in righteousness and truth.

You draw me in, under your wings, and hold me close.

Thank You, Father, for having a plan bigger than me. For having a heart bigger than any circumstance. For having a vision that wavers not, but pursues to the end.

Thank You for reminding me when I forget – if even for a moment.

"Surely your goodness and unfailing love will pursue me all the days of my life, and I will live in the house of the Lord forever." Psalm 23:6 (NLT)

When You Pray

"Seek the Kingdom of God above all else,
and live righteously,
and he will give you everything you need."
Matthew 6:33 (NLT)

If you could paint a picture or take a photograph to capture what prayer means to you, what would it look like?

My first thought is a young girl, head back, arms lifted high, standing in a field of grass. Storm clouds fill the sky around her, but a peaceful, gentle smile shines through her eyes as she gazes upward in loving trust.

I haven't always thought of prayer in this way; there have been many seasons and postures of prayer in my own life. Communion with God has taken on new and deeper levels of meaning as I've matured in Christ – as I've become freer to walk with Him as He desires – and I look forward to it expanding yet more.

Many good books have been written on prayer, exploring various types of intercession, meditation, purposes, and positions of entreating our Father. As I was reading in Matthew 6 this morning, however, I was struck again by the depth, yet simplicity, of Jesus' teaching on the topic.

First:

"When you pray, don't be like the hypocrites who love to pray publicly on street corners and in the synagogues where everyone can see them..." (v.5, NLT)

Does this mean we should do away with all public prayer? Is it wrong to pray aloud in church or to protest events with prayer rallies?

Not necessarily. As Jesus often did, He was addressing the condition of the heart in this verse. He was specifically pointing out those who pray with the underlying goal of being seen.

Pride can be a subtle issue. It slips in when and where we least expect it. We may think, "We're praying, after all. Isn't that enough?" But our Creator looks for humble and contrite hearts.

- Humility reveals an accurate understanding of God's authority and wisdom.
- Humility places its expectation on the One who's above all things, not in our own limited resources.
- Humility doesn't take away from our inheritance in Christ, but intensifies it as it positions us to be used by God.

On the other hand, when we pray just to be seen by others, we shift the focus to ourselves. In this place, we've lost sight of the exceeding privilege of agreeing with God.

Jesus warned: Those who pray from a position of pride receive only the temporal reward of man's attention. No other reward will be granted them from heaven.

Instead, Jesus encouraged His listeners to go into a private place, close the door, and pray to the Father who is in secret.

"Then your Father, Who sees everything, will reward you." Matthew 6:6 (NLT)

Our Father is not a hard-hearted master; He loves to reward His children. But He knows pride brings death into our lives and He will not reward us for something that dishonors Him and kills us.

Instead, His plan brings Life. His plan builds relationship.

Sooner or later, as communion with God in the secret place goes deeper, it will begin to flow out from under the door of our prayer closet and into the streets, even as the River of God flows out from under the temple door. (See Ezekiel 47:1-12.) But by then it will no longer be about us, but simply a pouring out of God through us.

Second:

> "When you pray, don't babble on and on as people of other religions do. They think their prayers are answered merely by repeating their words again and again." Matthew 6:7 (NLT)

Sometimes we think we have the answer and just need to convince God. That we see something He doesn't or have compassion He isn't feeling.

How blind we can be. God's mercy and loving-kindness far exceed our own. His wisdom and power cannot be measured or overcome. He is far above and beyond all things in love, purpose, and fortitude. For us to think our many words are what have caused God to pay attention is, again, a sign of pride and a shallow understanding of our Creator.

Verse 8 of Matthew 6 (NLT) speaks volumes:

> "…your Father knows exactly what you need even before you ask Him!"

And later, in verse 30,

> "And if God cares so wonderfully for the wildflowers that are here today and thrown into the fire tomorrow, He will certainly care for you."

So, why do we pray? Why do we ask?

Relationship – both to build it and to increase it.

That's why I picture the young girl as I described earlier in this post. She's in relationship with the One she is focused on. There may be storm clouds around her, but she's in perfect peace as she trusts in and relies on and agrees with her Maker. Her prayers become the sweet fragrance of worship and her petitions, the echoes of His heart. Her thanksgiving rises even before circumstances change because she knows He is doing much more than she could ever see or imagine – and all of it perfectly.

When you pray, remember, you are communing with the One who knows you and loves you more than you can imagine. He knows the intimate details of what happened yesterday and what will happen tomorrow. He loves to share His plans and to hear your voice agreeing with Him, to bring His Kingdom on earth.

This One sees what is in secret, even the secret places of our heart. May He find in us a heart being conformed to His.

Why I Believe

"For nothing is impossible with God."
Luke 1:37 (NLT)

Living where I do, surrounded by mountains, rivers, and wildlife, it's not hard to recognize the existence of our Creator.

- The wisdom of the changing seasons;
- the power of birth and regeneration;
- beauty and diversity beyond imagination.

God's fingerprints are everywhere.

But often, fingerprints in *unexpected* places convince us of His sovereignty even more.

Yesterday I had to do the thing I probably dislike most: buy a new laptop. It's not just the inconvenience or having to stretch this 47-year-old brain around new and updated programs. It's the whole process of buying a piece of equipment I use daily, but really don't have the knowledge or language to talk about with a salesman.

I don't know about processors or GB or resolutions. I'm not sure what speed or size or capacity I need. I just turn it on and write.

So, I did what I've always done when I needed a new computer: I called my younger brother, Cody. The same Cody who built my website and captured the amazing photos in my first book. He's my lifesaver.

After a dozen phone calls and visiting numerous websites and stores, I was finally ready to push the button.

The salesman on the other end of the line was very polite. He asked what kind of business I'm in and I told him I'm a writer and musician. We talked a bit more and he suggested a whole different model than I'd intended to order. This, of course, threw me into a tailspin; I needed to make a quick call (to Cody!) before making a decision.

This was no problem and the salesman sent me an email with the specs and a phone number for his direct line. "Oh, and what's the name of your book," he asked.

"*This Beloved Road*," I replied. "You'll find it at AmyLayneLitzelman.com." And we hung up.

A few hours, several phone calls to Cody, and a trip to the store later I called the salesman back. When I told him my name, he said, "Oh yeah, the author. Great website!"

Surprised he had taken time to check it out, I replied, "Thanks! My brother did a great job!"

"Oh, that too, but I mean the content. So many people don't get it. *There's such a bigger picture.*"

And we had a moment of sharing our faith in Jesus.

At the end of the call, he briefly went back to our earlier topic. "I'm sending you another email with *my* story. You'll see why going to your website meant so much to me."

And we said goodbye.

I clicked the link in his email and was immediately met with the smile of a beautiful lady. Underneath: her recent obituary. Left behind: a husband and young daughter.

- Only God knows the depths of sorrow and change this salesman is living through.
- Only the Holy Spirit could orchestrate a frustrated shopper who writes about God's power, love, and healing to call right when this salesman's line was open.

- Only the Creator of a perfectly ordered universe could bring together a need in Nashville, TN, with an encouragement in Jackson Hole, WY.

This is why I believe.

Why You Are Valuable

"Are not five sparrows sold for two cents?
Yet not one of them is forgotten before God.

Indeed, the very hairs of your head
are all numbered.

Do not fear;
you are more valuable than many sparrows."
Luke 12:6 (NASB)

What gives you your sense of worth?

This isn't a question we often ask ourselves outright, yet this crucial thread runs through every aspect of our thoughts and actions.

Maybe you believe you need to work hard and earn money to be of value. Maybe you're striving to perfect a talent, studying to gain more knowledge, or giving everything away and rearranging your life to help others.

Sadly, each of these thoughts and plans are often motivated by a deep, innate desire to be loved and accepted. And when you can no longer do what you believe gives you value, a cloud of worthlessness sets in.

My husband, Matt, and I are walking with a parent through the painful battle with cancer and more than once I've heard the quiet comment, "I'm just worthless. Worthless." With the physical body failing and strength and focus at a low point, this precious man believes his very existence is no longer valuable because he can't take care of himself.

While praying last night I came to the simple truth:

"May he know how much he's loved."

Isn't that the bottom line of our worth – that we're worthy of love?

Let's look for a minute at who Jesus placed value on. After all, He's our Creator. He's the one who'd know our true worth.

> "Now on the final and most important day of the Feast, Jesus stood, and He cried in a loud voice, If any man is thirsty, let him come to Me and drink!" John 7:37 (AMP)

Jesus shouted for *all* to hear. He cried out to *anyone* who was thirsty. He didn't give a list of qualifications or requirements. He invited all. He valued all.

But Jesus didn't just shout this invitation; He radically sought out those whose worth was questionable in the eyes of the world.

- The woman at the well, wife of five husbands and now living with another man.
- A fisherman who witnessed miracle after miracle, yet still denied he knew Jesus.
- Tax collectors betraying their own people for money from a corrupt government.
- The very man who would deliver Jesus to death on a cross.

Men and women who had failed again and again; Jesus extended a life of love to each one.

Your value has nothing to do with what you can and cannot do. Your worth isn't about being worthy. God values you far beyond your talent or gifting or goodness.

He loves you without the trappings of accomplishments or achievement.

God values you simply because you exist.

I love Ephesians 2:4-6. God loves you so much that *in order to satisfy His own great love* He offers you life, even while you're dead in sin and shame and failure. God loves you regardless of your circumstances. And in this great love, you're worth more than all the riches the earth can contain.

Just think:

> If pure, eternal, unconditional Love is the foundation on which you stand, even if all else falls away, you are still valuable because you are loved.

Today:

> "May you have the power to understand, as all God's people should, how wide, how long, how high, and how deep his love is.
>
> May you experience the love of Christ, though it is too great to understand fully. Then you will be made complete with all the fullness of life and power that comes from God." Ephesians 3:18-19 (NLT)

Willing to Be Filled

Something about a brimming pot grabs my spirit. It is eternally right for a vessel to fulfill its purpose.

It's now fall and I've been cleaning out flower pots and gardens. But thinking back over the last several months, I gained so much joy from digging and arranging, planting and dreaming.

Over the summer I'd often sneak away to the patio or front porch for mini-vacations. Containers overflowing with beauty and fragrance drew me to sit nearby where my soul found rest even as it soared. The life growing all around me echoed a call to be filled and flourishing.

In the same measure, an empty pot speaks to me of transition.

A dear friend of mine creates what she refers to as "message art" – miniature paintings of everyday items used by the Holy Spirit to frame a lesson in her journey. She often includes a few words to emphasize the point she learned.

A couple of years ago, sensing my place of transition and longing, she gifted me with one of her hand-painted cards. Clay pots overflowed with herbs and flowers, even as one container lay empty on its side. In the bottom corner was penned, "...*but available*."

What a beautiful image, this willingness to be filled. Empty, yes. But available.

I set the card on top of a bookshelf right inside my prayer room, where I'd see it often. Each time it caught my eye I would breathe, "*Yes, Father. Empty, but available.*" Just those words soothed my longing heart, knowing this transition would pass and take me to new places.

Seasons come and go. Summer doesn't last all year, but neither does winter. In the midst of transitioning from one place and time to another, we often feel empty and unfulfilled. Even a bit isolated and vulnerable. Here we get to the bottom of tough issues.

In our emptiness the Holy Spirit often tests our willingness:

- Am I willing to be used in ways I've never thought of?
- Am I willing to fulfill a destiny I don't yet know?
- Am I available to His plans and purposes?
- Am I available for more of God, Himself?

Did you realize God wants you to experience measures of His love you won't fully understand? Measures of love beyond earthly insight, but that complete and fill you with His very own life and power? Paul's prayer in Ephesians 3:16-19 (NLT) echoes the heart of a Creator willing to die to make this available:

> "I pray that from his glorious, unlimited resources he will empower you with inner strength through his Spirit.

Then Christ will make his home in your hearts as you trust in him. Your roots will grow down into God's love and keep you strong.

And may you have the power to understand, as all God's people should, how wide, how long, how high, and how deep his love is.

May you experience the love of Christ, though it is too great to understand fully. Then you will be made complete with all the fullness of life and power that comes from God."

If you feel empty, turn your heart forward. Don't look back in longing or despair, but ahead in anticipation and willingness. Rest, knowing this season is for a purpose as surely as the next will be.

At the perfect moment, God will fill you with Himself yet more, making you complete in new ways.

On the other hand, if you're overflowing with Christ's love and life, don't be surprised when others gather around you. Jesus is a perfect example of the magnetism of a vessel full of the Spirit.

Just as a brimming flower pot draws you to sit nearby, a brimming life also draws those longing for rest and joy. Those searching for peace and purpose.

Share your fruit.

Allow your leaves to be for healing.

Allow your destiny to be enjoyed by others.

Words on the Wind

"Plant your seed in the morning
and keep busy all afternoon,

for you don't know if profit will come
from one activity or another—
or maybe both."
Ecclesiastes 11:6 (NLT)

It's that time again. Dandelions!

Everywhere I look, yellow puff-balls adorn my yard. Almost instinctively I cringe. Then a smile sneaks across my face as I think back to dandelion necklaces as a young girl. What hours of fun!

Eventually, the yellow blooms will fade and tiny, white parachutes will transport seeds far and wide. It's not my favorite occurrence, but it always reminds me of a powerful principle: Seeds carry potential.

The most important seeds are the ones we sow with our words.

I love words – in all forms. I love to read them, sing them, and hear them spoken aloud.

Sometimes they go right over my head, when I'm busy or distracted. But then something catches my attention like a bur stuck on my sock and it just won't let go. A thought. A song. A comment. A bible verse. And before I know it a seed is planted.

I have a friend Bonnie. She radiates life everywhere she goes. I met Bonnie at a conference about nine years ago. She pulled out her djembe and played along as we led worship.

I'll never forget her dancing before the Lord, filling the room with her smile.

I soon learned Bonnie gives out scripture cards to most anyone who crosses her path. Over the years, I've accumulated a number of these precious 1x3 cards. They hang on my fridge, sit on the bedside table, and act as bookmarks in my bible. Their words have calmed storms, changed my course, and breathed Life into my soul:

>"The Lord will perfect that which concerneth me: thy mercy, O Lord, endureth for ever." Psalm 138:8 (KJV)

>"In the time of trouble he shall hide me in his pavilion: in the secret of his tabernacle shall he hide me." Psalm 27:5 (KJV)

>"If thou draw out thy soul to the hungry, and satisfy the afflicted soul; then shall thy light rise in obscurity." Isaiah 58:10 (KJV)

I can only imagine how many thousands of cards with Bonnie's fingerprints circle the planet. She is changing the world, one verse at a time.

Many dog-eared notecards and words of encouragement from friends surround my life. Hanging on cork boards in my office, strategically placed in drawers where I'll run across them, or in the change holder in my car. I also have countless notes I've written to myself.

All of these – seeds planted in my soul. Truths taking root as the Holy Spirit gives Life.

Precious words, shaping and molding my thoughts and life.

Never underestimate a note given or a word timely spoken. It may be in full bloom at that moment, or may lie dormant for years until the conditions are just right. Either way, like seeds on the wind, God-breathed words will always bring forth His Life.

What important words have others planted in your life? How do you release your seeds in the wind?

Worship: The Holy Exchange

"God is spirit,
and those who worship Him
must worship in spirit and truth."
John 4:24 (NASB)

Worship: When heaven meets earth
and earth embraces a Kingdom bigger than itself.

When my heart, my mind, my desires and circumstances
give way to the circumstances, desires, mind, and heart
of my King.

When my spirit exchanges weariness for Strength,
    despair for Hope,
    fear for Love,
    shame for Grace,
    guilt for Forgiveness,
    mourning for Joy,
    doubt for Courage,
    death for Life.

Jesus spoke of worship
when He taught the disciples how to pray:

    "Thy Kingdom come,
    Thy will be done,
    On earth as it is in heaven."

In the stillness of the night
when You whisper truths, deep to deep.

In the rush of daily life
when You lead and I follow, one step at a time.

When I catch glimpses of Your beauty and power
and my whole being is lost in You.

This perfect, eternal, Holy exchange
is worship that satisfies both heaven and earth:

> The Creator and the created – eternal harmonies
> of Love, Wisdom, and Power.

You Were Created to Plant Seeds, Not Build Monuments

"Plant your seed in the morning
and keep busy all afternoon,
for you don't know if profit will come from
one activity or another—or maybe both."
Ecclesiastes 11:6 (NLT)

One seed planted in the ground is worth far more than a bushel forever in the barn.

This thought has been ringing in my head for a while.

You see, I'm somewhat of a perfectionist. I've overcome the trap in many areas, but deep roots still linger in my writing.

How do I know?

Dozens of scribbled notes and partially finished posts tell the story. Nuggets of wisdom, joy, encouragement, and revelation received in simple, everyday ways, but put away in folders because my words didn't come together as well as I thought they should.

Desiring excellence is good. And striving for truth, important.

Trying to write *perfectly*, however, has often tied me in knots.

How about you?

- Any unfinished projects waiting for all of the pieces to come together?

- Maybe ideas or inventions that never got off the ground?
- Are your dreams lying dormant in unrealistic expectations?

In a desire for excellence, we often place the burden of perfection on ourselves and choke out the very gifts we long to give.

As I've wrestled with this, the Holy Spirit gave me His perspective:

All of life comes in seed form – not as monuments.

God created all living things to bring forth seed, not reproduce shrines.

I shouldn't expect what I do or create to ever be *completely* finished. Nothing is ever at a place where it cannot be added to or altered in some manner. Not because it's not good, but because God created life to be ever expanding.

My words shouldn't be trophies to look at, but seeds to continue the cycle of Life.

Look at Jesus. His words weren't meant to simply be plaques on a wall. His Life didn't end when He ascended to heaven.

Jesus spoke each word knowing they would bring forth Life. He knew all He said and did would continue to reverberate through the eternities. Not because of a shrine built in His honor or a Kingdom carved in stone, but because He reproduced His Life in others.

> "So will My word be which goes forth from My mouth; It will not return to Me empty, without accomplishing what I desire, and without succeeding *in the matter* for which I sent it." Isaiah 55:11 (NASB)

Every day you gather seeds: A word here, a picture there; a combination of colors, a unique intersection of lines, or the movement of light; a truth spoken in season or a breath of the Holy Spirit.

Gifts carrying creative Life.

Some will take root in your soul. They'll wash down in the cracks of your thoughts, break open, and start to grow. They'll always carry DNA from the original seed, but will now multiply and spread and take on a new form.

These broken down seeds will spring up in fields of green or as trees with sprawling branches. Fruit will ripen to feed you and all with whom you share. Life received. Life given.

The moment you try to perfect your fruit, however, its Life will begin to fade.

Don't try to build monuments. They are lifeless and eventually crumble. Instead, take the seeds you've gathered, the seed you've grown, and plant them. Plant them in words and paintings and math equations and generous acts. Plant them in recipes and inventions and a job well done.

Plant them knowing they may not be stared at or talked about or have photos taken of them by busloads of tourists. But they will bring forth new life. They will inspire and change lives and solve problems and bring joy.

Remember, one seed planted in the ground is worth far more than a bushel forever in the barn.

What do you have in your hand? It may be the very seed to change the world. Plant it and watch God work.

> "The rain and snow come down from the heavens and stay on the ground to water the earth. They cause the grain to grow, producing seed for the farmer and bread for the hungry." Isaiah 55:10 (NLT)

Endnotes

1   Tozer, A.W. 1961. *The Knowledge of the Holy*. New York, NY: HarperCollins Publishers, 1.

2   Litzelman, Amy Layne. 2010. *This Beloved Road*. Mustang, OK: Tate Publishing & Enterprises, LLC, 27.

3   Haskins, Minnie Louise. 1908. *The Desert*, "God Knows".

4   Litzelman, Amy Layne. 2010. *This Beloved Road*. Mustang, OK: Tate Publishing & Enterprises, LLC, 124.

5   Strong, James, LL.D., S.T.D. 1995. *The New Strong's Exhaustive Concordance of the Bible*. Nashville, TN: Thomas Nelson Publishers, Inc., 1105.

6   Strong, James, LL.D., S.T.D. 1995. *The New Strong's Exhaustive Concordance of the Bible*. Nashville, TN: Thomas Nelson Publishers, Inc., 1385.

7   Hattaway, Paul and Yun, Brother. 2002. Jordan Hill, Oxford: Monarch Books,,12.

8   Smith, Martin. 2011. *Delirious*. Colorado Springs, CO: David C Cook, 70.

9   Strong, James, LL.D., S.T.D. 1995. *The New Strong's Exhaustive Concordance of the Bible*. Nashville, TN: Thomas Nelson Publishers, Inc., G373.

10   Strong, James, LL.D., S.T.D. 1995. *The New Strong's Exhaustive Concordance of the Bible*. Nashville, TN: Thomas Nelson Publishers, Inc., G2663.

11   Litzelman, Amy Layne. "The Treasure Within Me".

12   A Kempis, Thomas. 1993. *The Imitation of Christ*. New York, NY: Catholic Book Publishing Corp., 5.